D0926366

Kids Learn!

Getting Ready for

8th Grade

Contributing Author

Chandra Prough, M.S.Ed.
National Board Certified Teacher

Publishing Credits

Conni Medina, M.A.Ed., *Managing Editor*; Robin Erickson, *Production Director*;
Lee Aucoin, *Creative Director*; Timothy J. Bradley, *Illustration Manager*;
Aubrie Nielsen, M.S.Ed., *Senior Editor*; Caroline Gasca, M.S.Ed., *Editor*;
Melina Sánchez, *Assistant Editor*; Marissa Rodriguez, *Designer*;
Stephanie Reid, *Photo Editor*; Rachelle Cracchiolo, M.S.Ed., *Publisher*

Image Credits

p. 6 istockphotography; All other images Shutterstock.

Teacher Created Materials

5301 Oceanus Drive
Huntington Beach, CA 92649-1030
http://www.tcmpub.com
ISBN 978-1-4333-2540-3
© 2014 Teacher Created Materials, Inc.

The classroom teacher may reproduce copies of materials in this book for classroom use
only. The reproduction of any part for an entire school or school system is strictly
prohibited. No part of this publication may be transmitted, stored, or recorded in any form
without written permission from the publisher.

Table of Contents

Índice de materias

Welcome to Kids Learn!

Dear Family,

Welcome to *Kids Learn! Getting Ready for 8th Grade*. Eighth grade will be an exciting year, with plenty of new educational opportunities. Your teen will study poetry and drama, learn about linear geometry, and master basic algebraic functions! Interesting new concepts in physics and American history will keep students engaged in lessons at school as well.

Kids Learn! was designed to help solidify the concepts your teen learned in seventh grade and help your teen prepare for the year ahead. The activities are based on the Common Core State Standards and provide practice with essential skills for the grade level. Keeping the skills your teen learned in seventh grade sharp while on break from school will help his or her eighth grade year get off to a great start. There is also a section at the end of the book that provides practice for standardized testing.

Keep these tips in mind as you work with your teen through the *Kids Learn!* book:

- Set aside a **specific time each day** to work on the activities.

- **Complete one language arts and one mathematics page** each time your teen works in the book rather than an entire week's worth of activity pages at one time.

- Keep all **practice sessions with your teen positive and constructive**. If the mood becomes tense or if either of you gets frustrated, set the book aside and find another time for your teen to practice.

- **Help your teen with instructions**, if necessary. If your teen is having difficulty understanding what to do, work through some of the problems together.

- Encourage your teen to do his or her best work and **compliment the effort that goes into learning**. Celebrate the completion of all the activities by filling in the certificate at the end of the book and displaying it in a special place.

Enjoy the time learning with your teen during his or her vacation from school. Eighth grade will be here before you know it!

Bienvenidos a Kids Learn!

Querida familia:

Bienvenidos a *Kids Learn! Getting Ready for 8th Grade*. El octavo grado será un año emocionante con bastantes nuevas oportunidades educativas para su hijo adolescente. Por ejemplo, ¡su hijo estudiará poesía y teatro, aprenderá sobre geometría lineal y dominará las funciones algebraicas básicas! Nuevos conceptos interesantes en física e historia estadounidense también mantendrán a los estudiantes involucrados en las lecciones escolares.

Kids Learn! fue diseñado para ayudar a consolidar los conceptos que su hijo aprendió en el séptimo grado y ayudar a su hijo a prepararse para el año que viene. Las actividades están basadas en los Estándares comunes del estado (*Common Core State Standards*) y proveen práctica con las destrezas esenciales para el nivel de ese grado. Mantener a punto las destrezas que su hijo aprendió en el séptimo grado mientras su hijo está de descanso de la escuela ayudará a que el año del octavo grado comience de gran manera. También hay una sección al final del libro que provee práctica para los exámenes estandarizados.

Tenga en cuenta estos consejos mientras completa junto con su hijo el libro *Kids Learn!*:

- Reserve un **tiempo específico todos los días** para trabajar en las actividades.
- **Complete una página de artes del lenguaje y una página de matemáticas** cada vez que su hijo trabaja con el libro, en lugar de completar al mismo tiempo las páginas de actividades que se completarían en una semana.
- Mantenga todas las **sesiones de práctica con su hijo positivas y constructivas.** Si el estado de ánimo se pone tenso, o usted o su hijo se frustran, ponga el libro a un lado y busque otro momento para que su hijo practique.
- **Ayude a su hijo con las instrucciones**, si es necesario. Si a su hijo se le dificulta entender qué hacer, completen algunos de los problemas juntos.
- Anime a su hijo a que haga su mejor esfuerzo y **elogie el empeño que se dedica cuando se aprende.** Celebre la terminación de todas las actividades llenando el certificado que se encuentra al final del libro y poniéndolo en un lugar especial.

Disfrute el tiempo en el que aprende con su hijo durante sus vacaciones de la escuela. ¡El octavo grado llegará antes de que se dé cuenta!

1. **Theme or central idea** of a text and how to analyze its development

2. **Meanings of words and phrases** as they are used in a text, including figurative and connotative meanings

3. **Informative, explanatory, narrative, and short** research projects

4. Radicals and integer **exponents**

5. **Proportional relationships**, lines, and linear equations

6. **Defining, evaluating, and comparing functions;** using functions to model relationships between quantities

7. **Motion, forces, and structure** of matter

8. Developing questions and **performing investigations**

9. Major events preceding the founding of the nation and their significance to the **development of America**

10. **Events from the Constitution up to World War I**, with an emphasis on America's role in the war

10

1. **Tema o idea central** de un texto y cómo analizar su desarrollo

2. **Significado de palabras y frases** que se utilizan en un texto, incluidos los significados figurados y connotativos

3. **Proyectos informativos, explicativos, narrativos y de investigación breve**

4. Radicales y **exponentes** enteros

5. **Relaciones proporcionales,** líneas y ecuaciones lineales

6. **Definición, evaluación y comparación de funciones;** uso de funciones para modelar relaciones entre cantidades

7. **Movimiento, fuerzas y estructura** de la materia

8. Desarrollar preguntas y **realizar investigaciones**

9. Acontecimientos importantes previos a la fundación de la nación y su significado para **el desarrollo de Estados Unidos**

10. **Acontecimientos desde la Constitución hasta la Primera Guerra Mundial,** con énfasis en el papel desempeñado por Estados Unidos en la guerra

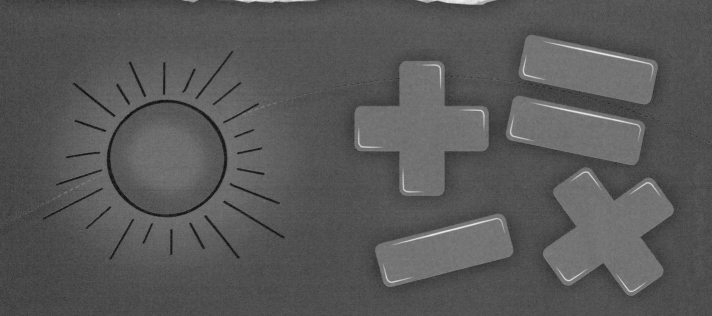

To Develop Healthy Habits

- Keep ahead of clutter by designating a specific time when everyone in the family is responsible for cleaning and organizing.

- Teens at this age still need about nine hours of sleep each night. Encourage your teen to engage in a relaxing activity before bedtime (e.g., a warm bath or a shower) and to avoid sleeping in on the weekends as this will interfere with weekday sleep patterns.

- Help your teen learn study and test-taking skills. Show him or her how to use a study guide, review notes, identify areas of weakness, read directions carefully, and monitor time during a test.

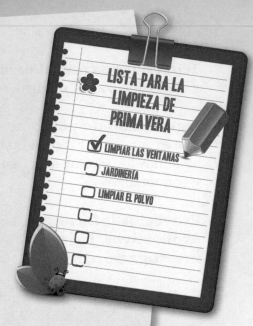

LISTA PARA LA LIMPIEZA DE PRIMAVERA

- ✓ LIMPIAR LAS VENTANAS
- ☐ JARDINERÍA
- ☐ LIMPIAR EL POLVO

To Practice Reading

- Establish a daily reading time of 15–30 minutes to read with your teen. Read selections out loud, discuss favorite scenes, look for evidence to support opinions, or analyze characters together.

- Encourage your teen to read a print or online newspaper every day. Review and discuss the headlines, photographs, editorials, and comics together.

- Start a vocabulary journal to note new and interesting words that you and your teen encounter in daily reading activities. Look up the new words in an online dictionary that provides audio of pronunciations. Write the words and their definitions in the journal, and then try to use the new words at least twice a week.

To Practice Writing

- Have your teen write a letter to a friend or relative. Review your teen's letter with him or her before mailing it to make sure complete sentences, capitalization, punctuation, and the proper letter format were used.

- Buy a notebook or diary for your teen and encourage him or her to make daily entries. Talk about the things you might write about in a diary and why.

- If you keep a vocabulary journal as suggested on page 8, ask your teen to pick a word, cut out a picture from a magazine or periodical that illustrates the word, glue it to a piece of paper, and write a sentence about the picture, using the word.

To Practice Math

- Ask your teen to pretend to redo a room in your house with new carpeting and paint. Have him or her measure the room, check local advertisements for price quotes and discounts, and compute the total cost based on how much carpet and paint is needed.

- Have your teen plan a menu for three family dinners with a total budget of $25.00. Tell him or her to check the food advertisements in the newspaper, add up the cost of the different items needed to make the three meals, and determine whether there will be any money left over.

- Ask your teen to help you determine the dimensions for a new tablecloth for your dining table. Have your teen measure the top of the table, determine how much fabric should hang over the edge of the table, and calculate the dimensions and surface area of the tablecloth.

Cosas para hacer en casa

Para desarrollar hábitos saludables

- Evite el desorden al establecer un tiempo específico en el que toda la familia es responsable de limpiar y organizar.

- Los adolescentes de esta edad todavía necesitan dormir alrededor de nueve horas todas las noches. Anime a su hijo a que haga una actividad relajante antes de la hora de dormir (p. ej., un baño cálido) y a que evite dormir demasiado tarde los fines de semana, ya que esto interferirá con los patrones de sueño de entre semana.

- Ayude a su hijo a aprender destrezas de estudio y técnicas para tomar exámenes. Muéstrele cómo usar una guía de estudio, repasar apuntes, identificar puntos débiles, leer instrucciones cuidadosamente y administrar el tiempo durante un examen.

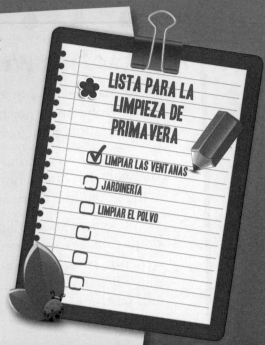

LISTA PARA LA LIMPIEZA DE PRIMAVERA

- ☑ LIMPIAR LAS VENTANAS
- ☐ JARDINERÍA
- ☐ LIMPIAR EL POLVO
- ☐
- ☐
- ☐

Para practicar la lectura

- Establezca un tiempo de lectura diaria de 15 a 30 minutos para leer con su hijo. Lean selecciones en voz alta, comenten sobre escenas favoritas, busquen evidencia para apoyar opiniones o analicen juntos los personajes.

- Anime a su hijo a que lea un periódico impreso o en línea todos los días. Juntos repasen y comenten los encabezados, las fotografías, las editoriales y las tiras cómicas.

- Comiencen un diario de vocabulario para anotar nuevas e interesantes palabras en un diccionario en línea que provee pronunciaciones en audio. Escriban las palabras y sus definiciones en el diario, y luego traten de usar las nuevas palabras al menos dos veces por semana.

© Teacher Created Materials

Para practicar la escritura

- Pida a su hijo que escriba una carta a un amigo o pariente. Revise la carta junto con su hijo antes de enviarla para asegurarse que usó oraciones completas, mayúsculas, puntuación y el formato formal para una carta.

- Compre un cuaderno o diario para su hijo y anímelo a que escriba entradas en su diario todos los días. Hablen sobre las cosas que escribirían en un diario y por qué.

- Si lleva un diario de vocabulario como se sugiere en la página 10, pida a su hijo que elija una palabra, recorte una imagen de una revista o un periódico que ilustra la palabra, la pegue a una hoja de papel y escriba una oración sobre la imagen usando esa palabra.

Para practicar las matemáticas

- Pida a su hijo simule que va a remodelar una habitación de su casa con alfombra y pintura nueva. Pídale que mida la habitación, revise anuncios locales para ver los precios y descuentos y que calcule el costo total basándose en cuánta alfombra y pintura se necesita.

- Pida a su hijo que planee un menú para tres cenas familiares con un presupuesto total de $25.00. Dígale que revise anuncios de comida en el periódico, sume el costo de los diferentes artículos que se necesitan para preparar las tres cenas y que determine si sobrará dinero.

- Pida a su hijo que le ayude a determinar las dimensiones para un mantel nuevo para la mesa del comedor. Pida a su hijo que mida la parte superior de la mesa, determine cuánto material debe colgar del borde de la mesa y que calcule las dimensiones totales y el área de la superficie del mantel.

To Develop Good Citizenship

- Have your teen think of a person in your community who exhibits good citizenship. Ask your teen to write a thank-you note to that person to honor that person's contributions to the community.

- Help your teen find information about the composting, recycling, and trash services available in your neighborhood. Have him or her make signs to post in community locations to educate people about the recycling opportunities available.

- Ask your teen to research charitable organizations in your community. Ask him or her to pick an organization and make a commitment to volunteer there monthly with you.

To Practice Reading

- When in the car, ask your teen to read the billboard advertisements. Discuss the meanings of the signs and the techniques used by the advertisers to sell their products.

- Go to the library on a regular basis. Explore a new section of the library with your teen and check out at least one book from the new section.

- Look for movies that are based on books and read the book with your teen before viewing the movie. After watching the movie, discuss the similarities and differences between the book and the movie and decide which version of the story each of you enjoyed more.

To Practice Writing

- Have your teen design and write a travel brochure detailing his or her favorite attractions in your community.

- Help your teen research and write a biography about the mayor of your city. Suggest that information be included about the mayor's past and also the mayor's plans for the future of your city.

- After eating at a restaurant, ask your teen to write a restaurant review. Make sure he or she includes factual information, such as the type of food served and the prices as well as his or her opinion of the food and service.

To Practice Math

- When shopping with your teen, point out sale signs and ask him or her to compute the amount of savings on an item. For example, if an item that normally costs $15.00 is 20 percent off, what is the savings?

- When planning an excursion or a short trip, ask your teen to consult a map to determine the shortest route, the approximate mileage, and the expected arrival time. Have your teen record the mileage on your car's odometer when you leave and then calculate the actual mileage when you reach your destination.

- Visit a bank and help your teen open a bank account. Determine how much money your teen will deposit, how much interest will be earned monthly, how much interest will be earned over the course of a year, and how the interest compounds.

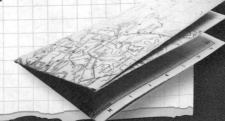

Cosas para hacer en la comunidad

Para ser un buen ciudadano

- Pida a su hijo que piense en una persona de su comunidad que demuestra ser un buen ciudadano. Pida a su hijo que escriba una nota de agradecimiento a esta persona para honrar sus contribuciones a la comunidad.

- Ayude a su hijo a encontrar información sobre el compostaje, reciclaje y servicios de recolección de basura disponibles en su vecindario. Pídale que haga letreros para poner en diferentes lugares en la comunidad para educar a la gente sobre las oportunidades de reciclaje disponibles.

- Pida a su hijo que investigue organizaciones caritativas en su comunidad. Pídale que elija una organización y que se comprometa a ofrecerse como voluntario junto con usted una vez por mes.

Para practicar la lectura

- Cuando estén en el carro, pida a su hijo que lea las vallas publicitarias. Comenten sobre los significados de las señales y las estrategias usadas por los anunciantes para vender sus productos.

- Vayan a la biblioteca a menudo. Explore una nueva sección de la biblioteca junto con su hijo y traten de pedir prestado al menos un libro de la nueva sección.

- Busquen películas que estén basadas en libros y lea el libro con su hijo antes de ver la película. Después de ver la película, comenten las similitudes y diferencias entre el libro y la película y decidan cuál versión de la historia le gustó más a cada quién.

Para practicar la escritura

- Pida a su hijo que diseñe y escriba un folleto de viajes que detalla sus atracciones favoritas en su comunidad.

- Ayude a su hijo a investigar y escribir una biografía sobre el alcalde de su ciudad. Sugiérale que incluya información sobre el pasado del alcalde y también sus planes para el futuro de la ciudad.

- Después de comer en un restaurante, pida a su hijo que escriba una crítica de restaurante. Asegúrese que incluya información relevante, como el tipo de comida que se sirve y los precios, así como su opinión sobre la comida y el servicio.

Para practicar las matemáticas

- Al estar de compras con su hijo, muestre letreros de rebajas y pídale que calcule la cantidad que se ahorraría en un artículo. Por ejemplo, si un artículo que normalmente cuesta $15.00 está a 20 por ciento de descuento, ¿cuánto se ahorrará?

- Al planear una excursión o una salida corta, pida a su hijo que consulte un mapa para determinar la ruta más corta, el millaje aproximado y la hora estimada de llegada. Pídale a su hijo que anote el millaje del odómetro del carro cuando salgan y que calcule el millaje real cuando lleguen a su destino.

- Visiten un banco y ayude a su hijo a abrir una cuenta de banco. Determinen cuánto dinero depositará su hijo, cuánto interés se ganará al mes, cuánto interés se ganará durante el transcurso de un año y cómo se calcula el interés.

Suggested Vacation Reading
Lectura sugerida para las vacaciones

These books are recommended for students in seventh and eighth grades. Most, if not all, of these books are available at your local library or bookstore. Encourage your teen to read daily and record his or her reading progress in the Vacation Reading Log on page 17.

Estos libros son recomendados para estudiantes de séptimo y octavo grado. La mayoría de estos libros, si no todos, están disponibles en su biblioteca local o librería. Anime a su hijo a que lea diariamente y registre el progreso de su lectura en el Registro de lectura de las vacaciones en la página 17.

Fiction

Hive Mind by Timothy J. Bradley
Rumble Fish by S. E. Hinton
Code Talker: A Novel About the Navajo Marines of World War Two by Joseph Bruchac
The Giver by Lois Lowry
My Side of the Mountain by Jean Craighead George
Lord of the Flies by William Golding
Little Blog on the Prairie by Cathleen Davitt Bell
A Separate Peace by John Knowles
The Witch of Blackbird Pond by Elizabeth George Speare
The Chosen by Chaim Potok
Anything But Typical by Nora Raleigh Baskin

Nonfiction

Night by Elie Wiesel
Freedom Riders: John Lewis and Jim Zwerg on the Front Lines of the Civil Rights Movement by Ann Bausum
Sugar Changed the World: A Story of Magic, Spice, Slavery, Freedom, and Science by Marc Aronson and Marina Budhos
The Diary of a Young Girl by Anne Frank
Bootleg: Murder, Moonshine, and the Lawless Years of Prohibition by Karen Blumenthal
The Hive Detectives: Chronicle of a Honey Bee Catastrophe by Loree Griffin Burns
10,000 Days of Thunder: A History of the Vietnam War by Philip Caputo
Tracking Trash: Flotsam, Jetsam, and the Science of Ocean Motion by Loree Griffin Burns
Good Brother, Bad Brother: The Story of Edwin Booth and John Wilkes Booth by James Cross Giblin

Vacation Reading Log
Registro de lectura de las vacaciones

Encourage your teen to complete this reading log to keep track of his or her vacation reading.
Anime a su hijo a completar este registro de lectura para llevar la cuenta de su lectura durante las vacaciones.

Date *Fecha*	Title *Título*	Number of pages *Número de páginas*

Language Arts Websites

Book Adventure
http://www.bookadventure.com
Book quizzes for many different books

Read, Write, Think
http://www.readwritethink.org/parent-afterschool-resources
Student materials that support literacy learning in the K–12 classroom

International Children's Digital Library
http://en.childrenslibrary.org
Online database of eBooks organized by age, reading level, language, genre, or interest

Vocabulary Games
http://www.vocabulary.co.il
Large collection of games to build and test vocabulary knowledge

Daily Grammar
http://www.dailygrammar.com/archive.html
Database of grammar lessons and quizzes covering parts of speech, parts of a sentence, and the mechanics of grammar

Mathematics Websites

Math Dictionary
http://www.amathsdictionaryforkids.com
An interactive online math dictionary for students

Figure This! Math Challenges for Families
http://www.figurethis.org
Math problems to challenge families

Funbrain
http://www.funbrain.com/brain/MathBrain/MathBrain.html
Fun, arcade-style games covering a variety of math concepts

SoftSchools.com
http://www.softschools.com/math
Math concepts, tips, games, and activity sheets

Education.com
http://www.education.com/activity/math
Suggestions for math games to make and play at home

En español

Mundo Latino
http://www.mundolatino.org
Base de datos extensiva para hispanohablantes con enlaces a diferentes temas, juegos educativos y revistas en la red

StoryPlace
http://www.storyplace.org/sp/storyplace.asp
Lo último en la biblioteca digital de los niños. Explore estas páginas llenas de cuentos para niños, jóvenes y adultos

¡Colorín Colorado!
http://www.colorincolorado.org
Información, actividades, y consejos para padres y maestros de estudiantes que hablan español

Aplicaciones Didácticas
http://www.aplicaciones.info/lectura/lectura.htm#peques
Base de datos de cuentos cortos y preguntas de comprensión correspondientes

Fun Educational Apps

Explor-eBook
Teacher Created Materials, Inc.
A library of hundreds of interactive eBook titles that offer engaging reading practice across grade levels and content areas

American History Timeline
McGraw-Hill School Education Group
Navigate the history of the United States and test your knowledge with interactive games

iSolveit: MathScaled
CAST, Inc.
Five levels of puzzles to promote an understanding of equations

Khan Academy
Khan Academy
Over 4,000 videos offering tutorials on a wide range of topics

18

#13540—Kids Learn! Getting Ready for 8th Grade

© Teacher Created Materials

Weekly Activities for Students

Actividades semanales para estudiantes

Tarzan of the Apes

Directions: Read the passage, then answer the questions on a separate sheet of paper.

Instrucciones: *Lee el pasaje, luego contesta las preguntas en una hoja de papel aparte.*

An excerpt from "Chapter I: Out to Sea" by Edgar Rice Burroughs

So it was that from the second day out from Freetown, John Clayton and his young wife witnessed scenes upon the deck of the *Fuwalda* such as they had believed were never enacted outside the covers of printed stories of the sea.

It was on the morning of the second day that the first link was forged in what was destined to form a chain of circumstances ending in a life for one then unborn such as has never been paralleled in the history of man.

Two sailors were washing down the decks of the *Fuwalda*, the first mate was on duty, and the captain had stopped to speak with John Clayton and Lady Alice.

The men were working backward toward the little party who were facing away from the sailors. Closer and closer they came, until one of them was directly behind the captain. In another moment he would have passed by and this strange narrative would never have been recorded.

But just that instant the officer turned to leave Lord and Lady Greystoke, and, as he did so, tripped against the sailor and sprawled headlong upon the deck, overturning the water pail so that he was drenched in its dirty contents.

For an instant the scene was ludicrous; but only for an instant. With a volley of awful oaths, his face suffused with the scarlet of mortification and rage, the captain regained his feet, and with a terrific blow felled the sailor to the deck.

The man was small and rather old, so that the brutality of the act was thus accentuated. The other seaman, however, was neither old nor small—a huge bear of a man, with fierce black mustachios, and a great bull neck set between massive shoulders.

As he saw his mate go down he crouched, and with a low snarl, sprang upon the captain, crushing him to his knees with a single mighty blow.

1. Why did the captain react to his fall with such anger?

2. Why did the large seaman react to the captain in the way he did?

Multiplying Rational Numbers

Directions: Find each product.

Instrucciones: *Encuentra cada producto.*

1. $(-7)(-2) =$ _____

2. $(-0.02)(0.007) =$ _____

3. $(-0.2)(-\frac{1}{2}) =$ _____

4. $(-5\frac{3}{5})(-1\frac{11}{14}) =$ _____

5. $(-3)(5)(-2)(1) =$ _____

6. $(4)(7)(-2)(-2) =$ _____

7. $(-0.3)(1.2)(-0.5) =$ _____

8. $(0.84)(3.15) =$ _____

9. $(-5\frac{5}{6})(6\frac{3}{7}) =$ _____

10. $(0.28)(9.51) =$ _____

11. What is the rule for multiplying signed numbers?

_____

_____

_____

Reading Comprehension: Story Elements

Directions: Read the passage, then complete the table below on a separate sheet of paper.

Instrucciones: Lee el pasaje, luego completa la gráfica de abajo en una hoja de papel aparte.

Saturday is the big championship game, and the fifth-grade soccer team is ready. The team has trained hard all year—they have practiced kicking, stopping, blocking, and shooting the ball. The players have listened to their coach and have carefully followed her instructions. As a result, they remain undefeated this year and are now playing in the championship game. Katherine and Becky are two of the team's star players. As a forward, Katherine's main job is to score, which is no problem with her powerful and accurate kick. Becky plays the very tough position of goalkeeper, whose job it is to block the opponent's ball from entering the goal. She is an excellent goalkeeper because she reacts quickly and is not afraid to dive and leap to block the ball. Katherine and Becky are sure they will win the championship game, but they are trying not to be overconfident. They continue to work hard at practice and to listen to the coach.

On game day, Katherine rushed for the ball as soon as the whistle blew. She passed the ball to Anita, who passed it to Emily, who passed it back to Katherine. Then Katherine moved her feet swiftly, dribbling the ball closer and closer to the goal. Soon she was in position—she shot for the net and scored! Her teammates leaped for joy as they cheered.

The opposing team was also good, however. The fifth-grade team led by one point near the end of the second half. With less than a minute remaining in the game, the opponents had the ball. It was up to Becky to save the game. If she blocked the ball from entering the goal, her team would be the champion. But if she didn't, then the other team could win. Becky kept her eyes focused on the ball, ready to block. Pop! The ball was up, and Becky dove toward it with her arms stretched out. She blocked the shot! The entire team ran toward Becky, exchanging high-fives all the way. They had won the big championship game!

Story Elements	
Characters: Who is involved? What are they like?	
Setting: Where is the action taking place? When is it taking place?	
Plot: Explain how the setting and characters influence the plot development.	
Theme: What is the central theme? Give examples of how the theme develops.	

© *Teacher Created Materials*

Dividing Rational Numbers

Directions: Find each quotient. Round decimal answers to the nearest hundredth.

Instrucciones: *Encuentra cada cociente. Redondea las respuestas decimales a la centésima más cercana.*

1. $\frac{7}{4} \div \left(-\frac{1}{7}\right) =$ _____

2. $-\frac{1}{2} \div -7 =$ _____

3. $\frac{4}{9} \div \left(-\frac{20}{75}\right) =$ _____

4. $13\frac{1}{2} \div (-6) =$ _____

5. $43.26 \div 6.7 =$ _____

6. $-\frac{8}{9} \div (-4) =$ _____

7. $4\frac{1}{8} \div 2 =$ _____

8. $\frac{2}{3} \div -\frac{1}{6} =$ _____

9. $265.97 \div 5.12 =$ _____

10. $-\frac{36}{6} =$ _____

11. Which is a better buy: a 12-pound bag of cat food for \$18 or a 15-pound bag of cat food for \$24? Justify your answer by showing the unit cost of each bag.

Topic Sentences

Directions: The topic sentence below is followed by a set of statements. Some of them are relevant to the topic, and some are not. Eliminate the irrelevant ones, and organize and restructure the rest into an effective paragraph on a separate sheet of paper.

Instrucciones: *La oración principal de abajo es seguida por un conjunto de enunciados. Algunos de ellos son relevantes y otros no. Elimina los que no son relevantes y organiza y modifica el resto en un párrafo efectivo en una hoja de papel aparte.*

Topic Sentence: The school week should be reduced to four longer days per week.

1. School is boring; it's just the same old thing every day, and there's so much homework.

2. My teachers each think their class is the only one we students have; they give us more homework than we can possibly do.

3. Personally, five days is just too long for me. I get burned out, and I think my teachers do, too.

4. My dad once had a four-day-per-week job, working ten hours per day.

5. We teens need more rest time since we're growing, and an extra day is all we ask.

6. Eight school hours for four days may be a bit too long, but we'll sacrifice for a longer weekend.

7. Teens are not adults yet, so we still need time to have fun and be with friends in a noneducational environment.

8. A four-day school week would really benefit teens.

Algebraic Expressions

Directions: Evaluate the expressions.

Instrucciones: *Evalúa las expresiones.*

Tip

Like terms have the same variables and corresponding exponents. Like terms in an expression can be combined. Unlike terms cannot be combined.

Los términos conexos *tienen los mismos variables y exponentes correspondientes. Los términos conexos en una expresión pueden ser combinados. Los términos no conexos no pueden ser combinados.*

Like Terms	Unlike Terms
$7x^2$ and $-3x^2$	$2y$ and $2x$
$8b$ and $3b$	$4a^3$ and $3a^2$

Part A

Combine like terms to simplify each expression.

1. $3y + y =$ _____

2. $b + b =$ _____

3. $5r - 2r =$ _____

4. $3c - 4c =$ _____

5. $\frac{2}{3}d + 3b + d =$ _____

6. $9x + 2y^3 - 4y - 6x =$ _____

7. $\frac{8}{2}x - 9y - 6x + 12y =$ _____

Part B

Evaluate the following expressions. Let $r = 3$ and $t = 9$.

8. $\frac{r}{t} =$ _____

9. $rt =$ _____

10. $\frac{r}{3} + \frac{t}{3} =$ _____

11. $r + t =$ _____

Part C

Evaluate the following expressions. Let $a = 5$, $b = -4$, and $c = 10$.

12. $ab =$ _____

13. $b + c =$ _____

14. $\frac{c}{5} =$ _____

15. $c - 5 =$ _____

$3x + 5 =$

What Would Change?

Directions: Imagine that the passage below was written from the point of view of the prince. How would it change the passage? Brainstorm a list of possible differences.

Instrucciones: *Imagina que el pasaje de abajo fue escrito desde el punto de vista del príncipe. ¿Cómo cambiaría el pasaje? Crea una lista de ideas de posibles diferencias.*

Excerpt from *The Prince and the Pauper*
by Mark Twain

Poor little Tom was in his rags. He was moving slowly past the sentinels. He moved with a fast-beating heart. He felt a rising hope. He saw a spectacle. It almost made him shout for joy. Within was a comely boy. The boy was tanned and brown by playing sturdy outdoor sports and exercises. His clothing was all of lovely silks and satins. It was shining with jewels. He had a little jeweled sword and dagger. He had dainty buskins on his feet. They had red heels. He wore a jaunty crimson cap. It had drooping plumes fastened with a great sparkling gem. Several gorgeous gentlemen stood near. They were his servants. He was a prince! A real prince. Tom knew it without the shadow of a question. The prayer of the pauper boy's heart was answered at last.

Tom's breath came quick. It was cut short with excitement. His eyes grew big. He felt wonder and delight. He had one desire. He wanted to get close to the prince. He wanted to have a good, devouring look at him. Soon Tom had his face against the gate bars. The next instant, one of the soldiers snatched him rudely away. He sent him spinning among the gaping crowd. The soldier said, "Mind thy manners, thou young beggar!"

The crowd jeered. They laughed. The young prince sprang to the gate. His face was flushed. His eyes were flashing with indignation. He cried out, "How dar'st thou use a poor lad like that? How dar'st thou use the King, my father's, meanest subject so? Open the gates. Let him in!"

Interpreting Data

Directions: The responses below were selected from random samples of women and men. Answer the questions about the data set.

Instrucciones: *Las respuestas de abajo fueron seleccionadas de muestras al azar de mujeres y hombres. Contesta las preguntas acerca del conjunto de datos.*

Question: How many hours did you spend watching television last week?

Responses from 10 women:

4, 1, 10, 15, 3, 6, 2, 7, 2, 9

Responses from 10 men:

5, 8, 10, 11, 14, 11, 6, 12, 15, 9

1. What is the mean number of hours the men spent watching television last week?

_____

2. What is the mean number of hours the women spent watching television last week?

_____

3. What inferences can you make about the television-viewing habits of women and men based on the data?

_____

_____

_____

_____

Understanding Poetry

Directions: Read the poem, then answer the questions.

Instrucciones: *Lee el poema, luego contesta las preguntas.*

The Courage That My Mother Had

The courage that my mother had

Went with her, and is with her still:

Rock from New England quarried;

Now granite in a granite hill.

The golden brooch my mother wore

She left behind for me to wear;

I have no thing I treasure more:

Yet, it is something I could spare.

Oh, if instead she'd left to me

The thing she took into the grave!

That courage like a rock, which she

Has no more need of, and I have.

—Edna St. Vincent Millay

---

1. What does the author inherit from her mother?

_____

2. How does she feel about this object?

_____

_____

3. What does the speaker mean by "Yet, it is something I could spare?"

_____

_____

4. What does the speaker wish she had inherited from her mother, and why?

_____

_____

5. What qualities do you feel your parents have passed down to you? Explain.

_____

_____

Calculating Percents

Directions: Solve the problems. Round all answers to the nearest whole number or percent.

Instrucciones: *Resuelve los problemas. Redondea todas las respuestas al número entero o al porcentaje más cercano.*

A local community club is offering tryouts for all interested students at its middle school basketball camp. Everyone is welcome.

1. You took 20 shots in your first workout and made 12 of them. What was your shooting percentage?

   $$20\overline{)120} \quad \frac{0.6}{120}$$

   $0.60 = 60\%$

2. Your best friend made 60% of the 40 shots he took. How many shots did your friend make?

3. Hi Lowe shot 35 times and made 25 shots. What was his shooting percentage?

4. Julie Shootsalott made 34% of her 50 shots. How many shots did she make?

5. Swish Malone took 28 shots and made 25 of them. What was his shooting percentage?

6. Slammin' Sammy made 95% of his 20 shots. How many shots did he make?

7. Lightning Lizzy made 34 out of 36 shots taken. What was her shooting percentage?

8. Your team made 44 of 68 shots in its first game. What was the team's shooting percentage?

Challenge: Compute your own shooting percentage from a game or a playground shoot-around. Indicate the number of shots taken, the number of shots made, and your shooting percentage.

Dress Code or No Code?

Directions: Should students have to wear uniforms to school? Make a claim in favor of or against school uniforms. Support your claim with logical reasons. Recognize different opinions, and include evidence against those claims.

Instrucciones: *¿Deberían los estudiantes usar uniformes en la escuela? Haz un argumento a favor o en contra de los uniformes escolares. Apoya tu argumento con razones lógicas. Reconoce las diferentes opiniones e incluye evidencia en contra de esos argumentos.*

The Maya

Directions: Read the passage, then answer the questions.

Instrucciones: *Lee el pasaje, luego contesta las preguntas.*

The Maya are one of the most interesting of the advanced civilizations that had developed in the Americas before the Spanish conquerors arrived in the early 1500s. They lived in what are now the countries of Guatemala, Honduras, El Salvador, Belize, and parts of Mexico. Most of their territory was only 200 to 600 feet above sea level and was covered with dense tropical forest. At the height of the Maya civilization, from around AD 300 to 800, they may have reached a population of about 2,000,000 people.

Today, many Maya ruins still lie buried in the dense growth of the tropical jungles. Not many of their ruins have been excavated and studied, but what we have learned from them tells us a lot about how these people lived. We have learned, for example, that they knew a great deal about astronomy and had developed a complicated calendar based on their study of heavenly bodies. They had also developed an advanced form of writing and a system of arithmetic. Their architecture and art are known and admired around the world.

The Maya were short and stocky with round heads, black hair, and brown skin. The men wore long loincloths, and the women wore long, straight skirts. In cold weather, they added blankets to their clothing for warmth. The clothes were often painted with designs and decorated with feathers. The common people lived in log huts that were scattered throughout the countryside and came to the cities when they had business there or to attend religious festivals. They grew and ate corn, beans, squash, sweet potatoes, and chili peppers. Their only domestic animal seems to have been the turkey. They kept bees for their honey.

The Maya built cities that were centers for religious festivals, markets, and government business, but as far as we know, no one lived there on a permanent basis. The temples, built on top of high stone pyramids, were the focus of urban activities. Only the priests mounted the steep stone steps to the tops of these pyramids; the people watched from below. The Maya practiced human sacrifice in these temples, but not to the same extent as the Aztecs who lived near what is now Mexico City.

1. This passage is mainly about

(A) the Mayan civilization from AD 300 to 800.

(B) the Mayan civilization after the Spanish invasion around AD 1500.

(C) the Mayan civilization before AD 300.

(D) the Mayan civilization after AD 900.

2. Why do you suppose no one lived in the cities?

(A) Living in the city was too expensive.

(B) They were not interested in art.

(C) Cities were used only for government, commerce, and worship.

(D) The people were afraid that they might be sacrificed in the temple.

Which Is More? Which Is Less?

Directions: Represent each group with ratios. Then, write an inequality to represent the answer to the question. Finally, answer the question in a sentence.

Instrucciones: *Representa cada grupo con proporciones. Luego, escribe una desigualdad para representar la respuesta a la pregunta. Finalmente, contesta las preguntas en una oración.*

1. Karla is in Group A, where 56 orange slices are shared equally among 7 people. Jade is in Group B, where 54 orange slices are shared equally among 6 people. Who had the greater share of orange slices, Karla or Jade?

2. Over a period of a week, the 4 people in Group C ran a total of 27 miles, while the 6 people in Group D ran a total of 39 miles. On average, who ran more miles—an individual in Group C or an individual in Group D?

3. Each of six groups evenly divides long strands of gum. Group E has 12 members and 29 cm of gum. Group F has 8 members and 18 cm of gum. Group G has 4 members and 11 cm of gum. Group H has 36 members and 105 cm of gum. Group I has 12 members and 32 cm of gum. Finally, Group J has 18 members and 39 cm of gum. The individuals of which group received the least gum?

4. A store sells prepackaged shrimp in 3 sizes. Bag K weighs 4 pounds and costs $15. Bag L weighs 5 pounds and costs $20. Bag M weighs 8 pounds and costs $25. Which is the best buy? Which is the worst buy?

32

 # 13540—Kids Learn! Getting Ready for 8th Grade

© Teacher Created Materials

Poetry Analysis

Directions: Read the poem aloud, and then answer the questions.

Instrucciones: *Lee el poema en voz alta y luego contesta las preguntas.*

The Road Not Taken

Two roads diverged in a yellow wood,
And sorry I could not travel both
And be one traveler, long I stood
And looked down one as far as I could
To where it bent in the undergrowth;

Then took the other, as just as fair,
And having perhaps the better claim,
Because it was grassy and wanted wear;
Though as for that the passing there
Had worn them really about the same,

And both that morning equally lay
In leaves no step had trodden black.
Oh, I kept the first for another day!
Yet knowing how way leads on to way,
I doubted if I should ever come back.

I shall be telling this with a sigh
Somewhere ages and ages hence:
Two roads diverged in a wood, and I—
I took the one less traveled by,
And that has made all the difference.

—Robert Frost

1. Analyze the form of the poem.

   a. How many stanzas does the poem have? _____

   b. How many lines are in each stanza? _____

   c. What is the rhyme pattern? _____

   d. How many beats are in each line? _____

2. Is there a regular rhythm to the poem, or does the rhythm vary? Give examples.

   _____

   _____

3. How do the structure and form of the poem relate to its meaning?

   _____

   _____

Identifying Expressions

Directions: Find the expression that matches each phrase. To answer the riddle below, write the letter in each blank space that matches the problem number.

Instrucciones: *Encuentra la expresión que concuerda con cada frase. Para contestar el acertijo, escribe la letra en cada espacio en blanco que corresponda al número del problema.*

1. A number added to 6	(D) $9 - n$
2. 10 decreased by a number	(R) $18 \div n$
3. 21 plus a number	(E) $21 + n$
4. A number divided by 18	(H) $10 - n$
5. Four times a number	(N) $n + 11$
6. Four times the sum of a number and two	(A) $4n$
7. 18 divided by a number	(Y) $n - 3$
8. A number minus 3	(O) $2n$
9. A number decreased by 10	(S) $6 + n$
10. 11 more than a number	(W) $n \div 18$
11. A number subtracted from 3	(G) $3 - n$
12. A number multiplied by 2	(I) $n - 10$
13. The sum of 9 and x	(T) $4(n + 2)$
14. The quotient of 9 and a number	(K) $9 \div n$
15. The product of 9 and a number	(U) $9n$
16. 9 less than n	(M) $9 + x$
17. A number subtracted from 9	(P) $n - 9$

Question: Why did the lady put lipstick on her head?

$\overline{}\ \overline{}\ \overline{}\quad \overline{}\ \overline{}\ \overline{}\quad \overline{}\ \overline{}\ \overline{}\ \overline{}\ \overline{}\ \overline{}$
 1   2   3   4   5   1   6   7   8   9   10   11

 6   12   13   5   14   3   15   16   2   3   7

 13   9   10   17.

It's All Greek (and Latin) to Me!

Directions: Use the information about the roots to determine the meaning of the underlined words.

Instrucciones: *Usa la información sobre las raíces para determinar el significado de las palabras subrayadas.*

1. Laniya's voice was barely <u>audible</u> over the roar of the crowd in the soccer stadium.

   What does the word *audible* mean? **Hint:** The Latin root *audi-* means *hearing, listening, sound.*

   _____

2. Throughout history there have been several <u>pandemics</u>, including smallpox, tuberculosis, and HIV.

   What does the word *pandemic* mean? **Hint:** The Greek root *pan-* means *all.*

   _____

3. Mr. Garza suffers from <u>insomnia</u>, so he is often tired during the day.

   What does the word *insomnia* mean? **Hint:** The Latin root *somn-* means *sleep.*

   _____

4. The <u>desolate</u> town hadn't been the same since the hurricane damage.

   What does the word *desolate* mean? **Hint:** The Latin root *sol-* means *alone, only.*

   _____

5. Select one of the Greek or Latin roots on this page. Think of another word that contains the root and write a sentence using the word.

   Word: _____

   Sentence: _____

   _____

   _____

   _____

Converting to Decimals

Directions: Convert each rational number to a decimal. Use long division to convert the fractions to decimals.

Instrucciones: *Convierte cada número racional a un decimal. Usa división larga para convertir las fracciones en decimales.*

A *rational number* is any number that can be expressed as a fraction. Any rational number can also be expressed as a decimal.

Un número racional *es cualquier número que puede expresarse como una fracción. Cualquier número racional también puede expresarse como un decimal.*

Examples/Ejemplos:

$3 = 3.0$

$4 = 4.0$

$\frac{1}{5} = 0.2$

1. $3\frac{3}{5} =$ _____

2. $8 =$ _____

3. $\frac{7}{8} =$ _____

4. $6\frac{1}{4} =$ _____

5. $\frac{9}{16} =$ _____

6. $4\frac{5}{9} =$ _____

7. $321 =$ _____

8. $\frac{2}{11} =$ _____

9. $\frac{9}{8} =$ _____

10. $\frac{65}{99} =$ _____

13540—Kids Learn! Getting Ready for 8th Grade
© Teacher Created Materials

Purpose and Viewpoint

Directions: Read the passage. On a separate sheet of paper, write short answers to the questions that follow.

Instrucciones: *Lee el pasaje. En una hoja de papel aparte, escribe respuestas cortas para las preguntas que siguen.*

Have you ever been to the zoo? What animals did you see? Have you noticed the monkeys? You should next time! Monkeys are extremely interesting animals.

Monkeys are among the most intelligent and lively animals in the world. Because of their playful nature, monkeys are very popular in zoos, where they are often people's favorite exhibit. There are many types of monkeys—about 200 in all! Most of them live in tropical areas such as Central and South America, Africa, and Asia. Many live in tropical forests, high up in the trees. Others live in grasslands called savannas.

Monkeys vary in size, shape, and color. Some monkeys are only about six inches long, whereas the tallest monkeys can be as long as 32 inches. Monkeys that live on the ground have shorter tails than monkeys that live in trees. Monkeys also have differently shaped noses. Some have nostrils that are close together, and others have nostrils that are spread apart. Their eyes are large and face forward, which helps them find food. The number and shape of their teeth also vary. Their hair can be white, orange, brown, gray, or black.

Monkeys have long arms and legs that help them climb trees and run, and their tails help them balance and hang from trees. You may have seen monkeys in zoos swinging from branch to branch using their arms, legs, and tails. It is quite amazing how well monkeys can move from tree to tree. Some can even grab objects with their tails. Monkeys have hands with opposable thumbs and feet with opposable big toes. These opposable thumbs and toes can be used with other fingers and toes to grab even the smallest objects.

Monkeys eat a variety of foods. They usually eat flowers, fruit, grass, and leaves. Lizards, frogs, insects, and birds' eggs may also be part of their diet. Depending on the type of food they eat, the structure of their teeth differs. Those that eat mainly leaves have sharp back teeth to shred the leaves.

Most monkeys live together in social groups, with anywhere from 20 to 100 members. Some even live in family groups. Baby monkeys stay very close to their mothers, who give them food and keep them safe. Monkeys in zoos are lively and always look as if they are playing and having fun, which is probably where the phrase "monkey around" came from.

1. What is the author's purpose for writing this passage?

2. How does the author feel about monkeys? Include quotations from the passage to support your statement.

Using the Pythagorean Theorem

Directions: Draw a picture for each problem, and include labels based on the information given. Write and solve the equation. Then, answer the questions.

Instrucciones: *Dibuja una imagen para cada problema e incluye etiquetas basándote en la información dada. Escribe y resuelve las ecuaciones. Luego, contesta las preguntas.*

Use the Pythagorean Theorem to find the missing sides of right triangles. The Pythagorean Theorem states $a^2 + b^2 = c^2$.

Usa el teorema de Pitágoras para encontrar los lados desconocidos de un triángulo rectángulo. El teorema de Pitágoras declara que $a^2 + b^2 = c^2$.

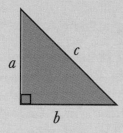

1. A ramp has a height of 7 feet and a horizontal base of 24 feet. What is the length of the inclined plane (the hypotenuse)?

2. What is the length of the diagonal of a rectangle whose height is 8 cm and whose base is 15 cm?

3. What is the height of a rectangle whose base is 40 inches and whose diagonal is 41 inches?

4. What is the distance across the lake?

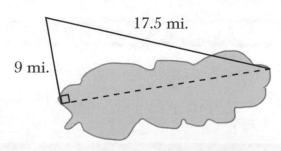

17.5 mi.

9 mi.

Idiomatic Expressions

Directions: Underline the idioms in each sentence. Then, write the sentence with the meaning of the idiom. Make sure that the word or phrase means the same as the idiom.

Instrucciones: *Subraya los modismos en cada oración. Luego, escribe la oración con el significado del modismo. Asegúrate de que la palabra o frase signifique lo mismo que el modismo.*

An *idiom* is an expression that has a meaning different from the meanings of the words themselves. For example, we may say, "Hold your horses," but what we really mean is "Wait—you are being impatient."

Un modismo *es una expresión que tiene un significado diferente del significado de las mismas palabras. Por ejemplo, nosotros podemos decir: "Para el carro", pero lo que realmente queremos decir es: "Espérate: estás siendo impaciente".*

1. The referee told the crowd to <u>pipe down</u>.

The referee told the crowd to be quiet.

2. At basketball practice, we can't get away with anything!

_____

3. When it comes to fighting, my dad puts his foot down.

_____

4. I wouldn't turn my nose up at the chance to wrestle him.

_____

5. Tia is supposed to audition for the musical tomorrow, but she is getting cold feet.

_____

6. Hudson blew his stack when he got a low score on his science test.

_____

7. My grandfather is as fit as a fiddle—and he's 104 years old!

_____

8. Mr. Gordon regretted buying the company; he lost his shirt on that deal.

What's the Unit Rate?

Directions: Complete the tasks below.

Instrucciones: *Completa las tareas de abajo.*

Stacy earns $4 for each dog she walks. She paid an initial $20 for supplies to use while walking the dogs. Create a table showing her profit for walking 2, 4, 6, 8, and 10 dogs. Use the middle column to show your work.

1.

Number of Dogs Walked (x)	Expression	Profit (in dollars) (y)

2. *Graph the data above. Plot the Number of Dogs Walked on the x-axis and the Profit on the y-axis.*

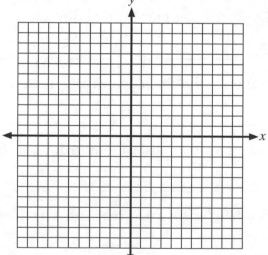

3. Write an equation to represent the problem.

_____

4. Which number in the equation represents the unit rate?

_____

Research Project

Directions: Choose a topic from history that is of interest to you. Develop a question about the topic to focus your research. Use several sources to research your question. Then, develop additional related questions to investigate.

Instrucciones: *Escoge un tema de historia que te interese. Desarrolla una pregunta sobre el tema para enfocar tu investigación. Usa varias fuentes para investigar tu pregunta. Luego, desarrolla preguntas para investigar preguntas adicionales que se relacionen.*

Research Topic: _____

Research Question: _____

_____

Source #1: _____

Summary of information: _____

_____

_____

Source #2: _____

Summary of information: _____

_____

_____

Source #3: _____

Summary of information: _____

_____

_____

Additional questions for research: _____

_____

_____

Anthropology

Directions: Read the passage, and then answer the questions.

Instrucciones: *Lee el pasaje y luego contesta las preguntas.*

Anthropology is the study of human beings. (*Anthrop* means "humans," and -*ology* means "study of.") It is concerned with all aspects of human development. Because of this broad approach, it is generally divided into two branches—cultural anthropology and physical anthropology.

Cultural anthropology is the study of people who are alive today, and it has traditionally focused on the societies of the world that have little technology. It is the study of the broad area of learned behavior occurring only among humans. A cultural anthropologist making a study of an Inuit village, for example, would study clothing, food, religious practices, and a wide range of Inuit behaviors.

Physical anthropology is the study of the biological features of humans. Physical anthropologists trace and follow the development of the bones and skulls that they find to put together the fascinating story of human variation and human development. Their study can include people who are alive today, but it often deals with people who lived and died long ago.

Because human beings are so complex, it is impossible to separate completely the subject matters of these two branches. The *biocultural* approach to anthropology, which combines the physical and the cultural features, offers the best overall look at human beings.

1. What is the topic of the selection?

   (A) cultural anthropology

   (B) physical anthropology

   (C) anthropology in general

   (D) anthropologists

2. Physical anthropology is concerned with

   (A) all aspects of human development.

   (B) the history of human biology.

   (C) food and religious practices.

   (D) the broad area of learned behavior.

3. The author takes the position that it is impossible to completely separate physical and cultural anthropology because

   (A) both branches deal with people who are alive today.

   (B) both branches deal with people who left only bones to study.

   (C) human beings are so complex.

   (D) human beings always have a culture.

13540—*Kids Learn! Getting Ready for 8th Grade*

© *Teacher Created Materials*

A Crafty Problem

Directions: The students at Allen Middle School are having a craft show on Thursday, April 17. Each grade level will create items to sell at the craft show. The items have to be completed by 7:00 A.M. on Wednesday, April 16. Your job is to calculate when each grade level should begin working. **Note:** This is not a leap year.

Instrucciones: *Los estudiantes de la escuela secundaria Allen van a tener una exhibición de artesanías el jueves, 17 de abril. Cada grado creará artículos para vender en la exhibición de artesanías. Los artículos tienen que estar listos para las 7 de la mañana el miércoles, 16 de abril. Tu trabajo es calcular cuándo cada grado debe comenzar a trabajar.* **Nota:** *Este no es un año bisiesto.*

March

S	M	T	W	T	F	S
						1
2	3	4	5	6	7	8
9	10	11	12	13	14	15
16	17	18	19	20	21	22
23/30	24/31	25	26	27	28	29

April

S	M	T	W	T	F	S
		1	2	3	4	5
6	7	8	9	10	11	12
13	14	15	16	17	18	19
20	21	22	23	24	25	26
27	28	29	30			

1. Each school day, the sixth-grade students can make 7 items for the show. Their goal is to submit 110 items. On which day should they begin working?

_____

2. On Mondays, the seventh-grade students can make 8 items. On the other school days, they can make 6 items. Their goal is to submit 125 items. On which day should they begin working?

_____

3. On Tuesdays, the eighth-grade students can make 5 items. On Thursdays, they can make 4 items. On the other school days, they can make 6 items. Their goal is to submit 130 items. On which day should they begin working?

_____

4. If the eighth-grade students want to submit 130 items and can make 7 items on Mondays, 6 items on Tuesdays, and 2 items on Fridays, on which day should they begin working?

_____

Exciting Introductions

Directions: Below is a list of topics. Write an interesting topic sentence that tells what you would like to say about each topic and that will make a reader want to read more. Be creative!

Instrucciones: *En seguida está una lista de temas. Escribe una oración principal interesante que diga lo que quieres decir sobre cada tema y que haga al lector querer leer más. ¡Sé creativo!*

It is important to introduce a topic in a clear and interesting way. A good topic sentence not only tells what the topic will be but also says something more about the topic or expresses a point of view.

Es importante introducir un tema de manera clara e interesante. Una buena oración principal no solo habla de lo que se trata el tema; también dice algo más sobre el tema o expresa un punto de vista.

Circle the better topic sentence:

Encierra con un círculo la mejor oración principal.

This is about vegetables.

In an ideal world, there would be no need for vegetables.

1. government

_____

2. high school

_____

3. cars

_____

4. sleep

_____

5. video games

_____

6. sports

_____

Presidential Numbers

Directions: Use the information in the graph to answer the questions.

Instrucciones: *Usa la información en la gráfica para responder a las preguntas.*

The single bar graph shows the number of electoral votes as of 2012 for each of the 10 most populated states. There are 538 electoral votes distributed among elected officials from the 50 states and the District of Columbia to officially vote for the president of the United States. It takes 270 electoral votes to win an election.

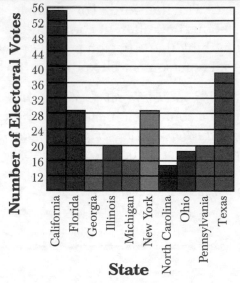

1. What is the interval between the numbers on the scale? _____

2. Write an equation to find the difference in the number of votes between Michigan and Illinois. _____

3. Write an equation to find the total number of electoral votes of the 10 most populated states. _____

4. How many electoral votes are distributed among the remaining 40 states and the District of Columbia? _____

5. If all 10 of these states voted for the same candidate, how many more votes would be needed to win a presidential election? _____

6. Write an equation to find which three states combined have the same number of electoral votes as California. _____

What's the Connotation?

Directions: Label each of the words below as either *positive* or *negative* to describe its connotation. Then, think of several word pairs that have similar denotations but different connotations.

Instrucciones: *Clasifica cada una de las palabras de abajo, escribiendo* positiva *o* negativa *para describir su connotación. Luego, piensa en varios pares de palabras que tienen denotaciones similares pero connotaciones diferentes.*

In writing, there are two different kinds of meanings of the words you use. The *denotation* of a word is its definition. The *connotation* of a word is the feeling or mental picture that people associate with the word. For example, the words *notorious* and *famous* have similar denotations but different connotations. *Notorious* has a negative connotation. It makes you think that a person is well-known for bad or outrageous things. *Famous* suggests that a person is well-known for the good things he or she did.

Al escribir, hay dos diferentes tipos de significado de las palabras que usas. La denotación *de una palabra es su definición. La* connotación *de una palabra es el sentimiento o imagen mental que las personas asocian con esa palabra. Por ejemplo, las palabras* notorio *y* famoso *tienen denotaciones similares pero connotaciones diferentes. Notorio tiene una connotación negativa. Te hace pensar que la persona es bien conocida por cosas malas y escandalosas. Famoso sugiere que la persona es bien conocida por las cosas buenas que hizo.*

1. _____ quickly/hastily _____

2. _____ debate/argument _____

3. _____ odor/fragrance _____

4. _____ snoop/investigate _____

5. _____ attract/lure _____

6. _____ call/yell _____

7. _____ mistake/oversight _____

8. _____ regretful/ashamed _____

9. _____ _____ / _____ _____

10. _____ _____ / _____ _____

© Teacher Created Materials

Using Formulas

Directions: Use the formulas for finding the circumference and diameter to answer the questions.

Instrucciones: *Usa las fórmulas para encontrar la circumferencia y el diámetro para contestar las preguntas.*

Formulas/Fórmulas

r: radius/*radio*　　　　　　　　　　*d*: diameter/*diámetro*

$r = \frac{1}{2}d$ and $d = 2r$　　　　　　$\pi \approx 3.14$

Formula for finding the circumference of a circle:
Fórmula para encontrar la circunferencia de un círculo:

$C = \pi d$

Formula for finding the area of a circle:
Fórmula para encontrar el área de un círculo:

$A = \pi r^2$

1. What is the circumference of this circle? _____

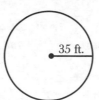

35 ft.

2. What is the area of this circle? _____

12 ft.

3. Give some examples, outside of school, where someone might need to find the area or circumference of a circle.

_____

_____

Writing Poetry

Directions: On a separate sheet of paper, write one quatrain and one cinquain. For help finding rhyming words, go to **http://www.rhymezone.com**. Type the word you want to find a rhyme for and select the Search button for a list of rhyming words.

Instrucciones: *En una hoja de papel aparte, escribe un cuarteto y una quintilla. Para ayuda en encontrar palabras que riman, ve a* **http://www.rhymezone.com**. *Escribe la palabra para la cual quieres encontrar una rima y pulsa el botón de busqueda para ver una lista de palabras que riman.*

A *quatrain* poem has four lines in each stanza. Lines 2 and 4 must rhyme. Lines 1 and 3 may or may not rhyme. Rhyming lines should have about the same number of syllables. You may write one or two stanzas.

A *cinquain* poem is about a person, a place, or a thing. A cinquain has five lines.

- Line 1 has one word that tells the subject of the poem (noun).

- Line 2 has two words that describe the subject (adjective).

- Line 3 has three words that describe something the subject does (action verb).

- Line 4 has four words that express feeling or describe the subject further.

- Line 5 has one word that is a synonym for the subject or sums up the poem.

Un poema de cuarteto *tiene cuatro versos en cada estrofo. Los versos 2 y 4 tienen que rimar. Los versos 1 y 3 no tienen que rimar, pero pueden. Los versos que riman deben tener el mismo número de sílabas. Puedes escribir una o dos estrofas.*

Un poema de quintilla *es sobre una persona, lugar o cosa. Una quintilla tiene cinco versos.*

- *El verso 1 se compone de una palabra que dice el sujeto del poema (sustantivo).*

- *El verso 2 se compone de dos palabras que describen el sujeto (adjetivo).*

- *El verso 3 se compone de tres palabras que describen algo que hace el sujeto (verbo de acción).*

- *El verso 4 se compone de cuatro palabras que expresan sentimiento o describen más al sujeto.*

- *El verso 5 se compone de una palabra que es un sinónimo para el sujeto o resume el poema.*

Bedroom Makeover

Directions: Use the information below to solve the problems.

Instrucciones: *Usa la información de abajo para resolver los problemas.*

The formula for the area of a rectangle:
La fórmula para encontrar el área de un rectángulo:
$A = lw$ (Area = length × width) or $A = bh$ (Area = base × height)

Background information:

- Wallpaper is sold in double rolls totaling 44 square feet.

- Carpeting is priced by the square yard.

- There are 9 square feet in 1 square yard.

- You cannot buy partial yards/rolls of carpeting or wallpaper.

Información adicional:

- *El papel para empapelar se vende en rollos dobles que equivalen a 44 pies cuadrados.*

- *Al alfombrado se le da precio por yarda cuadrada.*

- *Hay 9 pies cuadrados en 1 yarda cuadrada.*

- *No puedes comprar rollos parciales de alfombrado ni de papel para empapelar.*

1. Your mother said you could have new carpeting in your room if you compute the amount of carpeting needed and the cost. The length of your room is 18.5 feet and the width is 17 feet. The cost of a medium grade of carpeting is $20 per square yard.

a. How much carpeting will you need for your room?

b. How much will it cost to recarpet your room?

2. You want to cover one wall of your room with neon-color wallpaper that costs $25 for a double roll containing 44 square feet. The wall is 18.5 feet long and 10 feet high.

a. How much wallpaper will you need?

b. How much will the wallpaper cost?

Identifying Prepositional Phrases

Directions: Underline the prepositional phrase or phrases in each sentence.

Instrucciones: *Subraya la frase o las frases preposicionales en cada oración.*

> A *phrase* is a group of words that functions together like a single word but cannot stand alone as a sentence. *Prepositions* such as *about, at, by, on, for,* and *with* link words in a sentence. A *prepositional phrase* begins with a preposition and ends with a noun or a pronoun.
>
> *Una* frase *es un grupo de palabras que funcionan juntas como una sola palabra, pero que no pueden estar separadas en una oración. Las* preposiciones, *como* about, at, by, on, for, *y* with *unen las palabras en una oración. Una* frase preposicional *comienza con una preposición y termina con un sustantivo o un pronombre.*
>
> **Example:** We attended a concert <u>at the beach</u>.

1. The athletes with the top scores will advance to the next round.

2. Jacob checked out five books from the library.

3. Gina's cake with strawberries and cream was delicious.

4. Kayan wrote an essay about his experience at summer camp.

5. We drove through the mountains as we traveled to my aunt's house.

6. The deer hid among the trees as they waited for us to pass.

7. I need to study for the test until I understand the concepts.

8. We moved across the street from the high school.

9. After the earthquake, many people stayed in temporary shelters until the debris was cleared.

10. For some people, it's easier to identify prepositional phrases after memorizing common prepositions.

© *Teacher Created Materials*

Spin-O-Matic

Directions: Use a pencil to hold a paper clip in place in the center of the spinner. Spin the paper clip 50 times, and record the data in the table. Then, answer the questions.

Instrucciones: *Usa un lápiz para mantener un sujetapapeles en posición en el centro del círculo giratorio. Gira el sujetapapeles 50 veces y anota la información en la gráfica. Luego, contesta las preguntas.*

Spinner

Color	Number of Spins
Red	
Orange	
Yellow	
Green	
Blue	
Purple	

1. If you spin 50 more times, will you get the exact same results as above? Explain your reasoning.

   _____

   _____

2. Based on the data you collected, how many times would you expect to spin yellow in 500 spins? Explain your reasoning.

   _____

   _____

3. Based on the data you collected, how many times would you expect to spin red or blue in 1,000 spins? Explain your reasoning.

   _____

   _____

Narrative Conflicts

Directions: Think of conflicts you have experienced in each category below, and explain how each was resolved. Then, choose one conflict and compose a personal narrative on a separate sheet of paper. Include the circumstances and details of the conflict and the steps you took to resolve it.

Instrucciones: *Piensa en conflictos que hayas experimentado en cada una de las categorías de abajo y explica cómo cada uno se resolvió. Luego, escoge un conflicto y escribe una narrativa personal en una hoja de papel aparte. Incluye las circunstancias y los detalles del conflicto y los pasos que tomaste para resolverlo.*

One component of narrative writing is *conflict*. Conflict captures the reader's interest. Conflict is the problem or obstacle the character is trying to overcome.

Un componente de la escritura narrativa es el conflicto. *El conflicto capta el interés del lector. El conflicto es el problema u obstáculo que el personaje trata de superar.*

Person vs. Person

Conflict: _____

How the conflict was resolved: _____

Person vs. Machine

Conflict: _____

How the conflict was resolved: _____

Person vs. Nature

Conflict: _____

How the conflict was resolved: _____

Person vs. Self

Conflict: _____

How the conflict was resolved: _____

Person vs. Society

Conflict: _____

How the conflict was resolved: _____

Understanding Poetry

Directions: Read the poem. Apply the reading strategies below to help you understand the poem better. Then, answer the questions on a separate sheet of paper.

Instrucciones: *Lee el poema. Aplica las estrategias de lectura de abajo para ayudarte a entender mejor el poema. Luego, contesta las preguntas en una hoja de papel aparte.*

His Story

History lacks herstory
The essential fault is in
The pronoun

Kings, lords, warriors and knights, even
Explorers: all males
(some wearing mail,
some setting sail aboard ships named
after females.)

His-story lacks her-story
We-males need
Fe-males.
Prince Henry, Edward the First
Alex the Great, Peter the Worst

Where are the daughters?
Do we ignore the wives?
Just Xs on record—

So are there no Ys?
Please rewind
research
review
And relearn

Both sides of OUR-story
Give females their turn.
—*Author Unknown*

1. **Listen:** Listen to the rhythm of the poem as you read it.

2. **Look:** What images come to mind when you read this poem?

3. **Feel:** How does the poem make you feel?

4. **Look again:** Read each word one by one. Are there any hidden meanings? What are they?

5. **Look again:** What is the importance of the title?

6. **Listen again:** What is the poet saying? What is the message?

Cylinders and Cones

Directions: Find the volume of the cones and cylinders.

Instrucciones: *Encuentra el volumen de los conos y de los cilindros.*

Tip

In all of the formulas below,

r: radius   *h*: height $\pi \approx 3.14$

Cylinders

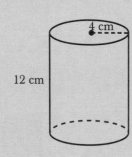

4 cm

12 cm

Cones

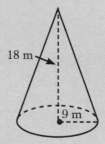

18 m

9 m

To find the volume of a cylinder, use the formula $V = \pi r^2 h$.

Para encontrar el volumen de un cilindro, usa la fórmula $V = \pi r^2 h$.

To find the volume of a cone, use the formula $V = \frac{1}{3}\pi r^2 h$.

Para encontrar el volumen de un cono, usa la fórmula $V = \frac{1}{3}\pi r^2 h$.

1. How much water will a cone-shaped cup hold if the diameter at the open end of the cup is 6 cm and the height is 9 cm? Draw a picture and show your work.

2. How much water will a cylindrical cup hold if the diameter of the cup is 6 cm and the height is 9 cm? Draw a picture and show your work.

3. How many cone-shaped cups would be needed to hold the same amount as a cylindrical cup? Explain how the answer is related to the formulas for finding the volume of cones and cylinders.

_____

_____

Compare and Contrast

Directions: Read the passage. On a separate sheet of paper, create a chart like the one below to compare and contrast different types of honeybees. Use a highlighter to cite evidence in the text that supports your comparisons.

Instrucciones: *Lee el pasaje. En una hoja de papel aparte, crea una gráfica como la de abajo para comparar y contrastar los diferentes tipos de abejas. Usa un resaltador para mostrar la evidencia en el texto que apoya tus comparaciones.*

Honeybees

Although there are about 20,000 kinds of bees in the world, honeybees are the most useful to people. They produce honey, which people use as food. They also produce beeswax, a substance that is used to make candles, crayons, and makeup.

Honeybees are social bees that live in groups called *colonies.* The colonies are inside hives, which might be boxes or hollow trees. The central structure of the colony is the wax comb, which is made up of six-sided, white wax chambers, or rooms. Some honeybee colonies have as many as 80,000 members. There are usually three types of bees in a colony—a queen, workers, and drones—and each type has a specific role to perform.

The queen's only job is to lay eggs. In the spring, the queen lays about 2,000 eggs a day! Each colony has only one queen, who may live for up to five years. If the old queen disappears or becomes feeble, a new queen is made. Sometimes, a young queen fights with an old queen until one stings the other to death.

A drone's job is to mate with the queen. There can be up to 500 drones in each colony. Drones are not able to hunt for food because their tongues are too short to suck nectar from flowers. So, they depend on worker bees to feed them. Drones live in the hive in the summer, but in the winter, worker bees may kick them out of the hive if there is not enough food.

Worker bees neither lay eggs nor mate. They spend their entire lives performing duties, or jobs. There are thousands of workers in a colony. At the beginning of their lives, workers clean the hive and feed other bees. Then, they produce wax and build honeycomb cells. Later, they protect the hive and eventually hunt for food. Workers hunt for food by sucking up nectar from flowers with their long tongues. Back in the hive, workers put the nectar in an empty cell, where it changes into honey. A worker bee can live from six weeks to several months.

People thousands of years ago ate honey that they stole from hives. Today, farmers keep hives of bees and sell the honey. Beekeepers have learned to handle their bees carefully. They wear special clothing, including veils to protect their faces. Thanks to the busy lives of bees, we can enjoy the sweet taste of honey and the glowing light of candles.

Types of Honeybees	Alike	Different
Queen/Drone		
Drone/Worker		
Worker/Queen		

Wordy Inequalities

Directions: Answer the questions. When possible, write and solve an inequality for each situation.

Instrucciones: *Responde las preguntas. Cuando sea posible, escribe y resuelve una desigualdad para cada situación.*

1. So far, Perry's Pet Shop has had $917.26 in purchases for the day. How much more must be sold for a total revenue of at least $1,200?

2. Carlos determined that his group needed to earn a profit of at least $1,780 with a series of fund-raisers such as car washes and spaghetti dinners. If the group spends $210 on supplies, what does the revenue need to be to reach the goal?

3. Madison wants to save at least $55 for a trip she will take in 4 weeks. If she saves the same amount each week, how much must she save per week to have at least $55?

4. Julia works as a waitress and is able to take home all of her tips. If she averages 16% tips on all meal checks, what must the total of all her customers' meal checks be for her to take home at least $200 in tips?

Rooting Around

Directions: Find the meaning of each word by combining the meanings of its parts from the chart. Write down your guess. Then, use a print or an online dictionary to verify the exact meaning.

Instrucciones: *Encuentra el significado de cada palabra combinando los significados de las partes en la gráfica. Escribe tu adivinanza. Luego, consulta un diccionario impreso o en Internet para verificar el significado exacto.*

Prefix		Word Root		Suffix	
dis-	*apart*	-mis-	*to send*	-al	*action*
com-	*together*	-plic-	*to fold*	-ate	*to make*
e-	*out*	-mot-	*to move*	-ion	*state*
in-	*not*	-cred-	*to believe*	-ible	*capable*
du-	*two*	-pos-	*to place*	-er	*a doer*
re-	*again*	-plex-	*to fold*	-ance	*condition*
		-son-	*to sound*		

1. commotion _____

2. mission _____

3. emotional _____

4. expose _____

5. commissioner _____

6. exposition _____

7. compliance _____

Any Way You Slice It

Directions: Determine which two-dimensional shape would be visible when each solid figure is sliced on the line indicated.

Instrucciones: *Decide cuál figura bidimensional se vería cuando cada figura sólida se divide en la línea que se indica.*

1.

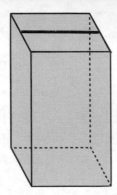

_____

2.

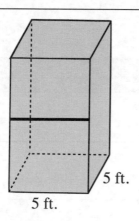

5 ft.
5 ft.

_____

3.

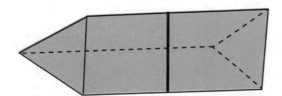

_____

4.

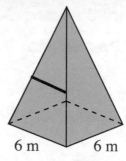

6 m   6 m

_____

5.

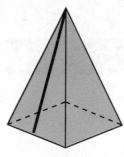

_____

6.

_____

     © Teacher Created Materials

Objectively Speaking

Directions: Read the passage, and then answer the questions.

Instrucciones: *Lee el pasaje y luego contesta las preguntas.*

When writing an *objective summary*, it is important to keep personal feelings out of the summary. An objective summary presents the facts without expressing an opinion about them.

Cuando escribas un resumen objetivo, *es importante dejar los sentimientos personales fuera del resumen. Un resumen objetivo presenta los hechos sin expresar una opinión sobre ellos.*

The Taj Mahal

In 1613, the emperor of India, Shah Jahan, was very unhappy because his beloved wife, Mumtaz Mahal, had died. Shah Jahan decided to build a tomb in his wife's memory. The tomb, known as the Taj Mahal or "Crown of the Palace," has become one of the most famous tourist sites in India.

During their life together, the couple had fourteen children. Mumtaz often went with her husband on military journeys. When Mumtaz died, Shah Jahan was grief-stricken. Legend says that his hair turned white overnight. Mumtaz had asked her husband to make a promise to build a tribute to their eternal love after her death. She also asked that he visit the tomb every year on the anniversary of her death.

Work on the tomb began in 1632. It took more than twenty years to build and 20,000 men to construct the palace-like tomb. The building is made of white marble and sits on a base of red sandstone. The supplies needed to build the tomb came from all over India and were transported to the area by 1,000 elephants.

There are tall towers, called minarets, standing 133 feet in height at each corner of the building and tilting slightly away. This design is so they will not fall on the tomb in the event of an earthquake. A huge dome made of precious stones was constructed over the center of the building. They make the tomb sparkle with different colors at different times of the day. They are pinkish in the morning, white in the evening, and golden colors when the moon shines. Sadly, the architect of the Taj Mahal was not rewarded well for his work. Stories say that Shah Jahan ordered all his fingers crushed to prevent him from ever designing a more beautiful building!

Today, the bodies of Shah Jahan and his wife lie beside each other in this monument to love. Some call the Taj Mahal the eighth wonder of the world.

1. Identify two central ideas in the passage.

a. _____

b. _____

2. On a separate sheet of paper, write an objective summary of the passage.

Operations with Integers

Directions: Write an equation to solve the problem. Then, answer the question with a complete sentence.

Instrucciones: *Escribe una ecuación para resolver los problemas. Luego, contesta la pregunta con una oración completa.*

1. The temperature when water freezes is 32°F. What temperature is 40° below freezing?

   Equation: _____

   Answer: _____

2. A golfer shot –4 (below par) on her first round of 18 holes. She shot –11 on her second round and –6 on her third round. How many shots below par was she after her three rounds?

   Equation: _____

   Answer: _____

3. The Acey Duecy Card Company owed the bank $1,000. They made a $750 payment to the bank. How much was still owed?

   Equation: _____

   Answer: _____

4. A contestant on a game show called *Double Trouble!* responded incorrectly to several questions, earning a score of –600 points. Then, he answered three questions correctly, earning 200 points, 100 points, and 150 points. How many more points does the contestant need to get back to zero?

   Equation: _____

   Answer: _____

5. The lowest temperature ever recorded was –128.6° F in Antarctica. The highest temperature ever recorded was 134° F in Death Valley, California. What is the difference between the temperatures?

   Equation: _____

   Answer: _____

Using Context for Vocabulary

Directions: Read each sentence or paragraph. Determine the meaning of the underlined word. Write down its meaning. Highlight the parts of the text that gave you clues about the word's meaning.

Instrucciones: *Lee cada oración o párrafo. Determina el significado de la palabra subrayada. Escribe su significado. Resalta las partes del texto que te dieron pistas sobre el significado de la palabra.*

1. "This is really important," said Margot. "If you <u>reveal</u> my secret, I will never be able to forgive you."

   Reveal means: _____

2. The tourists in the museum all gasped in admiration. "That painting is <u>exquisite</u>!" they exclaimed.

   Exquisite means: _____

3. "I cannot believe that your dog ate your homework again," said the teacher. "Your story is too <u>implausible</u>."

   Implausible means: _____

4. The boys were overjoyed to smell the aroma of pizza when they opened the front door. They were <u>ravenous</u> after a day without food.

   Ravenous means: _____

5. Instead of allowing one exception after another, our club decided to <u>amend</u> the rules to fit what we really allow.

   Amend means: _____

6. "I cannot eat parsnips," said Ryland. "They are the one vegetable that I really <u>abhor</u>."

   Abhor means: _____

7. After spilling water on the stickers, Brandye found that they would not <u>adhere</u> to the pages of her album.

   Adhere means: _____

8. Gabriel's grandma always reminded him not to <u>shirk</u> his responsibilities. She insisted that he complete his homework and his chores every afternoon before heading to the park to play basketball.

   Shirk means: _____

Mystery Drawings

Directions: Complete the chart. Use a ruler and protractor to draw the geometric figures according to the clues. Then, give the name of each figure.

Instrucciones: *Completa la gráfica. Usa una regla o un transportador para dibujar las figuras geométricas según las pistas. Luego, da el nombre de cada figura.*

Clues	Drawing	Name of Figure
1. I am a figure with three angles. All of my angles are equal.		equilateral triangle
2. I am a figure with three sides. My sides measure 2 cm, 5 cm, and 3 cm.		
3. I am a figure with three angles. My angles measure 140°, 20°, and 20°.		
4. I am a figure with three sides. Two sides measure 3 inches and one side measures 1 inch.		

The Day You Were Born

Directions: Find out what was happening in the world on the day you were born, and write a newsletter about that day on a separate sheet of paper. Your newsletter can be handwritten or typed. You might write an article about the most popular songs, movies, television shows, and books during the month or year you were born; an article about the newspaper headlines on the day you were born; a piece about what the weather was like; or an article about famous people who were also born on the same day as you were in earlier or later years.

Instrucciones: *Averigua lo que estaba pasando en el mundo el día que naciste y escribe un boletín informativo sobre ese día en una hoja de papel aparte. Tu boletín informativo puede ser escrito a mano o a máquina. Puedes escribir un artículo sobre las canciones, películas, programas de televisión y libros más populares durante el mes o año en que naciste, un artículo sobre los titulares del periódico el día que naciste, un escrito sobre qué tiempo hacía o un artículo sobre la gente famosa que también nació el mismo día que tú pero en años anteriores o posteriores.*

Library Reference Books

The library will have a variety of historical almanacs and yearbooks that include information about the day you were born on such topics as sports, current events, and statistics. The chronology of a year's events always appears in the next year's almanac. If you were born in 2000, for example, you would want to look in the almanac for 2001 to find out what happened in the year 2000.

La biblioteca tendrá una variedad de almanaques y anuarios que incluyen información sobre el día en que naciste en temas como deportes, sucesos del momento y estadísticas. La cronología de los eventos de un año siempre aparecen en el almanaque del próximo año. Así que, si naciste en el año 2000, busca en el almanaque del 2001 para averiguar lo que pasó en el año 2000.

Internet Sources

You can search for events during the year of your birth using any Internet search engine and typing in the year. One helpful website is **http://www.infoplease.com**. Enter the month, day, and year of your birth in the search field to find events that occurred in various categories.

Puedes buscar eventos del año de tu nacimiento al escribir el año en cualquier buscador de Internet. Algunos sitios web de gran ayuda incluyen: **http://www.informationplease.com**. *Pon el año de tu nacimiento en forma numérica en la búsqueda y encuentra eventos que ocurrieron en varias categorías.*

Bundle of Sticks

Directions: Read the passage, and then answer the questions on a separate sheet of paper.

Instrucciones: *Lee el pasaje y luego contesta las preguntas en una hoja de papel aparte.*

There once lived a merchant who was the proud father of three fine sons. However, the sons never stopped quarreling with one another. The father often told them how much easier life would be if they would work together, but they paid absolutely no attention to his advice.

Finally, their constant fighting became more than the merchant could bear, so he devised a plan to show them that they need to stick together. He called all his sons together and said, "My sons, the time is coming when I will no longer be with you. You will have to run the family business together and must learn to rely on one another. Yet the way the three of you fight, I cannot imagine you working together productively. So do this for me: gather a bundle of sticks, tie it with string, and bring it here."

When the sons returned with the bundle of sticks, the father said, "Take the bundle just as it is and break it in two. Whichever one of you can do that will inherit everything I own."

The eldest son tried first. He put his knee on the bundle and pressed and pulled with all his strength, but he could not bend the wood. Then, the middle son and finally the youngest son tried, yet each failed.

None of them could break the bundle. "Father, you have given us an impossible task!" they cried. The merchant nodded, then reached for the bundle, undid the string, and removed three sticks, handing one to each son.

"Now try," he said. All three sons easily snapped their sticks across their knees.

Then the merchant asked, "Now do you understand what I mean? When you work together, you will be strong and your business will prosper. But if you argue and go your separate ways, your enemies may break you."

1. What is the author's purpose for writing this passage?

2. Highlight or underline the clues in the text that led you to the author's purpose.

3. Describe the devices the author of this passage uses to express his or her point of view.

 # 13540—Kids Learn! Getting Ready for 8th Grade © *Teacher Created Materials*

Probability Practice

Directions: Make a diagram to determine the probabilities of the events occurring.

Instrucciones: *Haz un diagrama para determinar las probabilidades que tienen los eventos de ocurrir.*

> **Tip**
>
> The *probability* of a chance event occurring is expressed as a number between 0 and 1. The closer to 1, the more likely the event is to occur. The closer to 0, the less likely the event is to occur.
>
> *La* probabilidad *que tiene un evento al azar de ocurrir es expresada como un número entre 0 y 1. Lo más cerca de 1, lo más probable es que el evento ocurra. Lo más cerca de 0, lo menos probable es que el evento ocurra.*

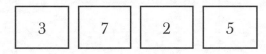

| 3 | 7 | 2 | 5 |

1. How many different 4-digit numbers can be formed from the four numbers above, using each digit only once?

   _____

2. What is the probability that the number 3 will be the first or third digit? Express the probability as a ratio, a fraction, and a percent.

   _____

3. What is the probability that the digits 7, 3, or 2 will be the last digit? Express the probability as a ratio, a fraction, and a percent.

   _____

4. Write and answer your own probability question for this problem.

   _____

   _____

   _____

   _____

Proposition and Support

Directions: Read two books or articles by different authors on the same topic. (For example: how to protect the environment or the importance of eating nutritious foods.) Then, complete the proposition-and-support chart, and answer the questions below.

Instrucciones: *Lee dos libros o dos artículos de diferentes escritores sobre el mismo tema. (Por ejemplo: cómo proteger el medio ambiente o la importancia de comer comida nutritiva). Luego, completa la gráfica de la proposición y apoyo y contesta las preguntas de abajo.*

Topic: _____

Title of book or article: _____		
Proposition: _____ _____		
Supporting Idea #1:	Supporting Idea #2:	Supporting Idea #3:

Title of book or article: _____		
Proposition: _____ _____		
Supporting Idea #1:	Supporting Idea #2:	Supporting Idea #3:

Analyze how each author presents key information. Do they emphasize different evidence? Do they interpret facts differently?

_____

_____

_____

    © *Teacher Created Materials*

Interpreting Graphs

Directions: Use the graphs of the proportional relationships to answer the questions.

Instrucciones: *Usa las gráficas de las relaciones proporcionales para contestar las preguntas.*

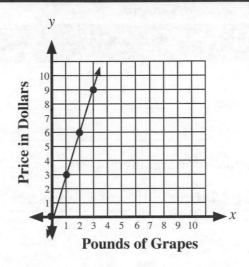

1.

   a. What does the point (0,0) represent on this graph?

_____

   b. What does the point (1,3) represent on this graph?

_____

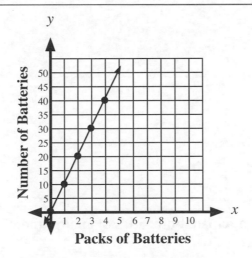

2.

   a. What does the point (0,0) represent on this graph?

_____

   b. What does the point (1,10) represent on this graph?

_____

Make Your Claim and Support It, Too!

Directions: Choose an issue about which you have a strong opinion. Propose a solution, and fill out the graphic organizer. You may need to do some research at the library or on the Internet about the issue you have selected.

Instrucciones: *Escoge un problema sobre el cual tengas una opinión firme. Propón una solución y completa el organizador gráfico. Quizás necesites hacer algo de investigación en la biblioteca o en Internet sobre el problema que escogiste.*

1. Make a claim about an issue: _____

   _____

2. List evidence for and against your argument:

Evidence Supporting Claim	Evidence Against Claim
A.	A.
B.	B.
C.	C.

3. Why is it important to anticipate both sides of an argument when planning an opinion piece of writing?

   _____

   _____

   _____

13540—*Kids Learn! Getting Ready for 8th Grade*
© *Teacher Created Materials*

In the Doghouse

Directions: Write an equation to represent the proportional relationship in the problem below, and then solve the problem.

Instrucciones: *Escribe una ecuación para representar la relación proporcional del problema a continuación y luego resuelve el problema.*

To build a single doghouse, Joey and Reece spend 1 hour and 20 minutes preparing and cutting pieces of wood, 40 minutes sanding the wood, 50 minutes assembling the doghouse, and 40 minutes painting the doghouse.

1. How long would it take the two friends to build six identical doghouses?

2. After Joey goes home, Reece decides to build three more doghouses on his own. How long will it take him?

Mythological Allusions

Directions: Use the information in the box to determine the meanings of the sentences. Write the literal meaning of each sentence.

Instrucciones: Usa la información en el cuadro para determinar el significado de las oraciones. Escribe el significado literal de cada oración.

Cupid was the Roman god of love.

Hercules was a hero in Greek mythology who was known for his courage and strength.

According to Greek mythology, **Pandora** was the first woman on Earth. She was given a box and told not to open it. She (or perhaps her husband) did open the box, releasing evil into the world.

Achilles was a warrior of Greek mythology who was shielded at birth by being dipped in the River Styx. The only part of his body that remained vulnerable was his heel (the place where he was held when he was dipped in the river). He was ultimately struck by an arrow in that unprotected spot.

1. The firefighters showed Herculean effort as they stormed into the burning building and rescued the people trapped inside.

   _____

   _____

2. Quinn usually eats healthy foods, but her Achilles heel is chocolate.

   _____

   _____

3. Renee knew her friend Raj wanted to go to the dance, so she played Cupid and set him up with her friend Lana.

   _____

   _____

4. The museum curator thought a painting might be a fake, and her investigation opened up a Pandora's Box of illegal activity among museum officials.

   _____

   _____

13540—Kids Learn! Getting Ready for 8th Grade   © Teacher Created Materials

It's a Rational Problem

Directions: Solve each problem.

Instrucciones: *Resuelve cada problema.*

1. An 18-ounce jar of peanut butter costs $3.78 while a 22.5-ounce jar of peanut butter costs $4.05. Which jar of peanut butter is the better buy? Use unit cost to justify your answer.

2. Byron eats 7.2 ounces of dark turkey meat. The meat is about 9.8% fat. How much fat did Byron consume?

3. Peter answered 86% of a 50-question test correctly. How many correct answers did he give? How many answers were incorrect?

4. Cheena bought 6 pounds of apples at $1.14 per pound and 24 small oranges at $0.26 each. What was the total cost?

Summer in the City

Directions: Read the passage, and then answer the questions.

Instrucciones: *Lee el pasaje y luego contesta las preguntas.*

Imagine a hot, summer day. The sun beats down on the blacktop, and the city air rises up in a zigzag. Light bounces off the cars parked on the street. The only sound heard is the steady hum of fans laboring to cool residents from the sweltering temperatures.

Bored children decide to brave the humid heat and play ball in the streets. Thump! Thump! Thump! The repetitive sound of a basketball breaks the monotonous silence. The children weave in and out, in and out, jumping, moving, dodging, and laughing as they move effortlessly, making plays in the hot summer rays.

Spewing a nerve-jangling tune, an ice cream truck arrives on the scene. The kids race excitedly over to the truck and select treats—vanilla cones, chocolate crunch bars, and wildly colored ice pops. The treats are quickly devoured, and the kids return to their energetic play.

Dark storm clouds roll ominously through the sky overhead, and the street empties. A gloomy grayness envelops the sky like a giant umbrella. Craaack! Thunder roars with anger after lightning dances fleetingly in the distance. The rain comes in torrents, beating, beating, beating down on the sidewalks, streets, and houses. Faces peer curiously out windows, observing the dazzling show. When the clouds roll away, steam rises, drying the streets for another round of play.

1. Which of these is a simile?
   A Bored children decided to brave the humid heat and play ball in the streets.
   B A gloomy grayness envelops the sky like a giant umbrella.
   C Faces peer curiously out windows, observing the dazzling show.
   D Imagine a hot, summer day.

2. Gloomy grayness is an example of
   A a simile.
   B a metaphor.
   C personification.
   D alliteration.

3. Which literary device is *not* used in this passage?
   A alliteration
   B simile
   C metaphor
   D repetition

4. The children in this passage are probably
   A very chilly.
   B in school.
   C on summer vacation.
   D inside.

13540—Kids Learn! Getting Ready for 8th Grade

© Teacher Created Materials

More Fun with Algebraic Expressions

Directions: Simplify each expression. Write the final answer in standard form.

Instrucciones: Simplifica cada expresión. Escribe la respuesta final en la forma estándar.

1. $4x - 8x + 5y - 10y =$ _____

2. $4m - 7m - 3n + 3m =$ _____

3. $2m - 3(3m - 7) =$ _____

4. $11x - 20y - (3x - 6) =$ _____

5. $5a - 3b - 5(3a - 4b) =$ _____

6. $-3(-2x + 7y) - (2y - 3x) =$ _____

7. $4c + 6d - 10c - 5d =$ _____

8. $8k + 4k - 3(5k + 6) =$ _____

9. $-4m - 7m - 4(2m + 7) =$ _____

10. $-4(5x - 6y) - (4x - 9y) =$ _____

11. $3r^2 + 2r - 12r^2 + 6r =$ _____

12. $12x^2 + 4(4x - 3) - 14x^2 =$ _____

Get Creative!

Directions: Plan a piece of fictional writing. Use a separate sheet of paper to plan characters, setting(s), and the plot. Write the first two paragraphs of your piece below, and then continue on another sheet of paper. Remember, you want to hook your readers with your first few sentences.

Instrucciones: *Planea un ensayo de escritura ficticia. Usa otra hoja de papel para planear los personajes, el escenario(s) y la trama. Escribe los primeros dos párrafos de tu ensayo abajo y luego continúa en otra hoja de papel. Recuerda, debes cautivar a tus lectores con tus primeras oraciones.*

The Bear and the Two Travelers

Directions: Read the passage and make inferences to answer the questions.

Instrucciones: *Lee el pasaje y haz deducciones para contestar las preguntas.*

This is a fable of two men who were traveling together, walking through the woods on their way to a final destination. Suddenly, a bear appeared before them on their path and frightened them.

Man 1: I didn't think twice but climbed quickly into a tree to save myself by hiding in the branches.

Man 2: I followed my fellow traveler but tripped. Knowing that I would soon be attacked, I remained on the ground, motionless.

Man 1: From my safe spot, I watched the bear as he felt the man lying on the ground, smelling him and nuzzling him all over with his snout.

Man 2: I held my breath and pretended to be dead.

The bear soon left, for it is said a bear will not touch a dead body. When the bear was definitely gone, the other traveler descended from the tree and jokingly asked his friend a question.

Man 1: What was it the bear whispered in your ear?

Man 2: He gave me this advice: Never travel with a friend who deserts you at the approach of danger.

The moral of this fable is: Misfortune tests the sincerity of friends.

1. Why do you think the first man climbed the tree and didn't help his friend?

   _____

2. How do you think the second man felt about his friend making a joke once they were out of danger? Why?

   _____

   _____

3. How might this experience have changed the friendship between the two men?

   _____

   _____

Temperature Changes

Directions: Write an equation for each problem, model it on the number line, and answer the question.

Instrucciones: *Escribe una ecuación para cada problema, ejemplifícala en la línea numérica y contesta la pregunta.*

Tip

Subtracting a rational number is the same as adding its additive inverse. The distance between two numbers on a number line is the absolute value of their differences.

Restar un número racional es lo mismo que sumar su aditivo inverso. La distancia entre dos números en una línea numérica es el valor absoluto de la diferencia.

Example:

$20 - (-10)$ is the same as $20 + (+10)$, which equals 30. This can be shown on a number line.

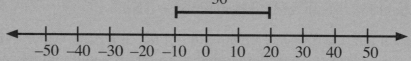

1. What is the temperature change if the temperature drops from 34°F to −7°F?

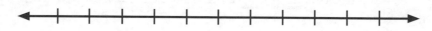

_____

2. What is the temperature change if the temperature drops from −4°F to −21°F?

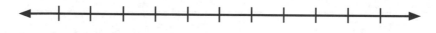

_____

3. What is the temperature change if the temperature rises from −23°F to 4°F?

_____

 © *Teacher Created Materials*

Creating a Summary

Directions: Read the passage, and then complete the tasks below.

Instrucciones: *Lee el pasaje y luego completa la asignatura de abajo.*

The Roof of the World

What is it like to stand on the roof of the world? I am lucky enough to know. On the Plateau of Tibet, 15,000 feet (5,000 m) above sea level, you truly feel as if you were standing on the roof of the world. The green and yellow plains, covered by low grasses, are surrounded by tall, snow-capped mountains. Over everything is the sky, which seems so much bigger and more light filled than anywhere else.

This plateau is the heart of the great Asian land mass. While most of it is in Tibet, now ruled by China, it extends into India, Nepal, and Bhutan. It is home to the world's highest mountains and the source of Asia's great rivers. On the southern edge are the Himalayas, including Mount Everest, known as *Chomolungma*, or "Goddess, Mother of the World," in the Tibetan language.

Sitting on this vast plateau are enormous glaciers; great sheets of ice cover hundreds of square miles. In the spring and summer, when some of the ice melts, it trickles down from the heights of Tibet. The water forms streams that run together to make great rivers.

These rivers travel in all directions, bearing life-giving water to all parts of the great continent. The rivers flow over the plains, bringing water for people to drink, for farmers to water their herds, and to flood rice paddies. Fish are raised in it, and crops are grown in it. The rushing waters also provide power for hydroelectric plants, bringing electricity to millions of people.

The rivers are a watery highway system on which people can travel. The first cities in Asia grew along these rivers, which were some of the earliest cities anywhere in the world. The great empires of Asia sprang from these cities, and with them came the great contributions of Asian science and culture.

It was while standing on the roof of the world, at the source of those rivers, that I decided to write this book. I wanted to tell the story of Asia by following three of its great rivers: the Huang He (also called the Yellow River), the Mekong, and the Ganges. I hope you, the reader, will come with me as I travel down these rivers and see the many wonders along their banks. It is a journey I have taken more than once, and one I want to share with you.

1. Reread the first paragraph. Identify and highlight the most important information. Look at what you have highlighted and develop one sentence that summarizes its most important ideas. Write it on a separate sheet of paper.

2. Reread the remaining paragraphs, stopping after each paragraph to develop a summary sentence for that paragraph. Add these to your first summary sentence.

3. Using your summary, determine the central ideas in this text.

Investigating One-Step Equations

Directions: Keira and Malia each solve four equations, but they have different answers. Check each equation and determine who is correct. Circle the correct answer for each equation.

Instrucciones: *Keira y Malia resolvieron cada una cuatro ecuaciones, pero tienen respuestas diferentes. Verifica cada ecuación y decide quién tiene la respuesta correcta. Encierra con un círculo la respuesta correcta para cada una.*

1. Equation: $x - 0.4 = 1.2$ Keira: 1.6   Malia: $\frac{4}{5}$

2. Equation: $x + \frac{4}{5} = 0.5$ Keira: $-\frac{3}{10}$ Malia: $\frac{13}{10}$

3. Equation: $0.4x = 1.2$ Keira: $\frac{24}{25}$ Malia: 3

4. Equation: $\frac{x}{0.3} = 5.1$ Keira: 17   Malia: 1.53

5. Explain how you know your answer for number 4 is correct.

_____

_____

_____

Evaluate an Author's Arguments

Directions: Read the passage, then evaluate the author's claims on a separate sheet of paper.

Instrucciones: *Lee el pasaje y luego evalúa las afirmaciones del autor en una hoja de papel aparte.*

Editorial: You CAN Make a Difference

By now, the majority of Americans realize that climate change is a big problem. Yet the problem seems so huge that the average citizen feels there is nothing he or she can do. In fact, individual actions, when taken by 300 million Americans, can make a huge difference in cutting carbon emissions and slowing global warming.

Here are some simple things you and your family can do to reduce the amount of carbon dioxide that is released into the atmosphere. Even if you just do one or two, you'll be doing your part to protect Earth and save our climate.

- **Wear hand-me-downs.** Every item of clothing you own has an impact on the environment. By wearing a family member's old T-shirt, you avoid consuming all the energy used to produce and ship a new one.

- **Ride the bus.** Almost 90 percent of all trips in the United States are made by car. Public transportation saves an estimated 1.4 billion gallons of gas each year.

- **Say no to plastic bags.** The next time your parents go to the store, help them pack the groceries in reusable cloth bags. Every year, more than 500 billion plastic bags are distributed, and fewer than 3 percent are recycled.

- **Open a window.** Instead of running the air conditioner, let in some fresh air. Set the thermostat higher in the summer and lower in the winter.

- **Take a cool shower** to reduce your use of energy-hogging hot water.

- **Plant trees, especially in tropical forests.** This plays a crucial role in cooling the planet. One tree can absorb up to a ton of carbon dioxide over its lifetime.

- **Reduce, reuse, recycle.** Look at making small changes to recycle cans, paper, and glass. Avoid using disposable objects like paper plates, cups, and towels. Some 900 million trees are cut down each year to make pulp and paper. People can decrease this number by buying recycled paper.

1. Does the author use factual claims or commonplace assertions and opinions? How do you know?

2. Are the pieces or evidence relevant and sufficient? What is the weakest claim, and how could the author have supported it better?

Graphing Inequalities

Directions: Solve the problem. Then, graph the inequality.

Instrucciones: *Resuelve el problema. Luego, grafica la desigualdad.*

1. Randy has a coupon for 20% off any purchase at Great Stuff, with a maximum discount of $15. What is the highest purchase price that will receive the full 20% discount?

a. Write an inequality to help you solve the problem.

b. Graph the solution on a number line.

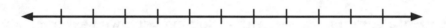

2. Sophia plans to spend $52 on some new clothes at Great Stuff. There is an 8% sales tax on her clothing purchase. She also picks up a few packs of gum for $0.99 each. If Sophia has $60 to spend, what is the greatest number of packs of gum she can buy?

a. Write an inequality to help you solve the problem.

b. Graph the solution on a number line.

Central Ideas in a Text

Directions: Read the passage. Identify the central ideas and write a summary.

Instrucciones: *Lee el pasaje. Identifica las ideas centrales y escribe un resumen.*

A Tasty Treat, a Poison . . . and an Argument?

Can you imagine a vegetable that can be made into a delicious filling for a pie or can be a poison? That's exactly the case with a vegetable called rhubarb. This sounds amazing, but it's true!

Rhubarb is often mistaken for a fruit because it is usually baked in a pie and eaten as a dessert. In fact, another name for rhubarb is *pieplant*. When rhubarb is combined with strawberries, raspberries, and apples, the flavor only gets better. Rhubarb is packaged in supermarkets in several ways. It comes in fresh stalks, frozen packages, or cans.

The rhubarb plant has large, green leaves on long, thick stalks. Some leaves are as large as two feet across. The stalks may be about an inch wide and can grow up to two feet long. The part of the rhubarb plant that people can eat is the red, juicy stalk. Eating the leaves may make someone ill. They contain oxalic acid, which is a poison.

The leaves of a rhubarb plant appear early in the spring. In cold climates, rhubarb is often the first sign of spring. Sometime later, the plant produces large flowers and seeds. Unlike most vegetables, the seeds from a rhubarb plant are not usually used to grow new plants because the seed does not always grow into exactly the same kind of plant it came from. To grow a new rhubarb plant, farmers cut pieces of the root and buds. Then, they plant those pieces in the ground. That way, the farmer knows that the new rhubarb plant will be similar to the plant from which it was cut. A rhubarb plant can live five to eight years.

The word *rhubarb* has several meanings. Dictionaries first define rhubarb as "an edible plant." The slang definition is given as "a heated argument, squabble, or fight." Some dictionaries link the original slang term to baseball, meaning a dispute between the players and an umpire.

1. What are the two central or main ideas of the text?

_____

_____

_____

2. Write an objective summary of the text on a separate sheet of paper.

Probability Solving

Directions: Solve the problem and show your work. You may wish to use a tree diagram or another strategy to help you.

Instrucciones: *Resuelve el problema y muestra tu trabajo. Quizás quieras usar un diagrama de árbol u otra estrategia para ayudarte.*

1. If 2 number cubes are rolled, what is the probability of rolling the sums below? Complete the table.

Sum	Probability
2	
3	
4	
5	
6	
7	
8	
9	
10	
11	
12	

2. Roll two number cubes 50 times. Complete the table with your results.

Sum	Tally of times rolled	Outcome
2		
3		
4		
5		
6		
7		
8		
9		
10		
11		
12		

3. Compare your results in Problem 2 to the probabilities you found in Problem 1.

_____

_____

_____

Characters and Plot

Directions: Read the passage, and then complete the tasks on a separate sheet of paper.

Instrucciones: *Lee el pasaje y luego completa las tareas en una hoja de papel aparte.*

Happenings at the Airport

Kristina's family was going to visit her grandparents. Kristina was very excited. However, on the drive to the airport, the streets were crowded with cars and they got stuck in traffic. They arrived at the airport very late. When they checked in, the attendant looked up and shook her head sadly. "You checked in too late," she said, "so we had to give your seats to other people. Now the plane is completely full."

The attendant booked them on another flight, which would leave two hours later. The family was upset, but all they could do was wait.

After two long hours, the family finally got on the plane. When they got off the plane after the quick flight and went out to the front of the airport, Grandpa and Grandma greeted them with huge smiles. Grandpa took Kristina's hand, and they happily chatted and laughed as they went together to pick up the luggage.

The sun was setting as they pulled into her grandparents' driveway. Everyone was starving and exhausted, so Grandpa quickly fixed up a tasty meal that everyone ate. When they were all full and rested, Grandma pulled out a board game, and they played for the rest of the evening. Even though the day was full of mishaps, they were happily together. "This is why trips are so much fun!" Kristina said.

1. Describe the plot (the action that happens in the story).

2. Describe the conflict (problem or main dilemma).

3. Describe the rising action (events that lead to the climax).

4. Describe the climax (action at its greatest point).

5. Describe the resolution (how the problem is solved).

6. Describe how the characters affect the plot.

More Inequalities

Directions: Solve the problem below as an inequality. Show your work.

Instrucciones: *Resuelve los problemas de abajo como desigualdades. Muestra tu trabajo.*

1. Karel must do some reading over a long weekend. He must read part of a 220-page book. For other classes, he also needs to read a 32-page chapter and a 30-page chapter. His goal is to read at least a total of 150 pages. Assume that Karel will read his shorter assignments first.

   a. At least what percent of the 220-page book must he read to accomplish his goal?

   b. If Karel reads the minimum number of pages, how many pages of the book must he read over the long weekend?

2. Create your own inequality problem and solve it.

   _____

   _____

   _____

   _____

Let's Dialogue

Directions: Write a short narrative about an interesting experience from your life. Practice using dialogue to move the story along. Remember to use correct punctuation for dialogue (e.g., quotation marks). A new paragraph should be used each time the speaker changes.

Instrucciones: *Escribe una narrativa corta sobre una experiencia interesante de tu vida. Usa diálogo para avanzar la historia. Recuerda usar puntuación correcta para el diálogo (p. ej., comillas). Un nuevo párrafo debe comenzar cada vez que el hablante cambia.*

Preparing Your Teen for Assessments

Background for Parents

Many states have recently adopted the Common Core State Standards, a set of national educational standards in language arts and mathematics. These standards provide clear goals for learning in grades K–12 so that all students can gain the skills and knowledge they need to be successful. For more information on the Common Core State Standards, please visit **www.corestandards.org**.

Assessments that are aligned with the Common Core State Standards will replace other state end-of-year tests. These assessments include a variety of types of items. Some items ask students to select the correct option or options from a list. Other items ask students to give a written or numerical response. Students will also complete tasks that gauge their ability to bring together knowledge and skills across many standards.

Preparation Pages

The test preparation items on pages 88–102 provide sample test questions and tasks similar to those that may be found on next-generation assessments. Use the following tips to work through the assessment practice pages with your teen:

- Work with your teen as he or she completes the practice items so that you can address any questions as they arise.

- Help your teen understand how to go about selecting answers or working through tasks.

- Use the Answer Key to check the answers together, and discuss any incorrect responses.

- Keep in mind that for the purposes of this practice, getting the correct answer is not as important as helping your teen become comfortable with the test-taking format and process.

© Teacher Created Materials

Preparar a su hijo para las evaluaciones

Información general para los padres

Muchos estados recientemente han adoptado los Estándares comunes del estado *(Common Core State Standards)*, un conjunto de estándares educacionales nacionales en artes del lenguaje y matemáticas. Estos estándares proveen metas claras para el aprendizaje en los grados K–12 para que todos los estudiantes puedan lograr las destrezas y el conocimiento que necesitan para ser exitosos. Para más información sobre los Estándares comunes del estado, por favor visite **www.corestandards.org**.

Las evaluaciones que se ajustan con los Estándares comunes del estado tomarán el lugar de otras pruebas de fin de año del estado. Estas evaluaciones incluyen una variedad de tipos de problemas. Algunos problemas les piden a los estudiantes que escojan la opción correcta u opciones de una lista. Otros problemas les piden a los estudiantes que den una respuesta escrita o numérica. Los estudiantes también completarán tareas que miden su habilidad para unir el conocimiento y las destrezas de muchos estándares.

Páginas de preparación para pruebas

Los problemas de preparación para pruebas en las páginas 88–102 proveen ejemplos de preguntas de pruebas y tareas similares a las que puedan encontrarse en las evaluaciones. Use los siguientes consejos para completar las páginas de preparación para pruebas con su hijo:

- Trabaje junto con su hijo mientras completa los problemas de práctica para que cuando surja cualquier pregunta pueda tratar con ella.

- Ayude a su hijo a entender cómo escoger las respuestas o completar las tareas.

- Use la Hoja de respuestas para juntos revisar las respuestas y analizar cualquier respuesta incorrecta.

- Tenga en cuenta que para los propósitos de esta práctica, obtener la respuesta correcta no es tan importante como ayudar a que su hijo se sienta cómodo con el formato y el proceso de evaluación.

Language Arts Assessment Practice

Directions: Read the passage, then answer the questions.

Jumpin' Johnny

Tall, skinny, imposing—that's how Johnny's friends would describe him. Johnny's blond hair was always spiked up with a bit of gel so that it would stay in place all day. He wore the latest fashion: a gigantic T-shirt, baggy shorts, and expensive athletic shoes. What the girls liked best, though, were his sparkling blue eyes that always suggested mischief.

Johnny was a powerhouse on the basketball court, too. Some say he could make a shot from a thousand feet away. His agility enabled him to leap, dodge, and dance down the basketball court.

In action, he was a gazelle, moving effortlessly toward his destination. On the court, his friends called him "Jumpin' Johnny." He earned this name because he would soar through the air about 10 feet, slam the ball into the net, and land on his feet. Then he would race down the court for the next play.

At home, "Jumpin' Johnny" was neither mischievous nor leaping, jumping, or dodging. He helped his little sister with homework. He also assisted with setting the dinner table and mowed the lawn every weekend during the summer. He loved history and would spend hours every evening reading about famous battles and former presidents of the United States. But when one of his friends called, Johnny once again assumed his school personality. He would talk, laughing and joking to show that he didn't take life too seriously. After all, he knew that the following day would bring more mischief and adventure.

1. Underline **two** sentences from the passage above that support the idea that "Jumpin' Johnny" was responsible and helpful.

     © *Teacher Created Materials*

Language Arts Assessment Practice *(cont.)*

2. Read the sentences from the passage and the directions that follow.

> He would talk, laughing and joking to show that he didn't take life too seriously. After all, he knew that the following day would bring more mischief and adventure.

Provide the central idea of the entire passage and describe how the sentences above fit into the passage's central idea.

_____

_____

_____

_____

_____

_____

3. Read the statement and the directions that follow.

> "Jumpin' Johnny" was an excellent basketball player.

Give two details from the text that support this conclusion.

_____

_____

_____

Language Arts Assessment Practice (cont.)

4. Read the sentence from the passage and answer the question that follows.

> But when one of his friends called, Johnny once again <u>assumed</u> his school personality.

What does the word *assumed* mean as used in the sentence above?

_____

_____

_____

5. Read the sentence and the directions that follow.

> In action, he was a gazelle, moving effortlessly toward his destination.

Choose **two** reasons why the author may have chosen to use the metaphor above.

- (A) It establishes the need to protect a gazelle's destination.
- (B) It helps the reader get a picture of Johnny in his or her mind.
- (C) It gives the reader a sense of Johnny's gracefulness on the basketball court.
- (D) It makes the reader smile to think of Johnny as a gazelle.

90

#13540—Kids Learn! Getting Ready for 8th Grade

© Teacher Created Materials

Language Arts Assessment Practice (cont.)

Directions: Read the passage, then answer the questions.

Is There Life Beyond Planet Earth?

Astronomers revealed a new lead in the search for extraterrestrial life in May 2007. For the first time, they discovered a planet outside our solar system that could possibly sustain life.

The planet is named Gliese 581c and was found by the European Southern Observatory. "It's a significant step on the way to finding possible life in the universe," says Michel Mayor. He is one of the 11 European astronomers on the team that discovered the planet.

The planet has Earthlike temperatures. Yet the star it orbits, known as a red dwarf, is much smaller than our sun. Astronomers do not yet know if there is liquid water on Gliese 581c. "Liquid water is critical to life as we know it," says Xavier Delfosse, an astronomer on the discovery team.

An Infinite Universe

Gliese 581c is located 120 trillion miles from Earth, so we may never know for sure whether life exists there. However, it seems that life in some form may exist elsewhere in the universe. As early as the 1950s, scientists performed related experiments. They showed that amino acids, the building blocks of proteins, could be formed by lightning strikes in the right kind of atmosphere. More recent discoveries suggest that the conditions that led to life on Earth could easily occur on other planets.

We certainly seem to want to believe there are other forms of life in space. As recently as the early 20th century, respected astronomers such as Percival Lowell said that the "canals" on Mars were built by some kind of intelligent life form. Today, we know that there are in fact no canals at all. They are merely an optical illusion.

There is new evidence that even on Mars, there was once water. Water is believed to be one of the conditions needed for life. In an infinite universe, with an infinite number of planets and stars, how could the simple reactions that lead to life happen in only one place?

At the same time, because the universe is so vast, we may never be able to visit another star system. It is also doubtful that we will ever pick up radio signals from other intelligent species. While some of us may be sure that life is out there, we will probably never know for sure.

Meanwhile, scientists will keep searching. They will keep studying planets like Gliese 581c. Maybe, just maybe, scientists will one day look into space and find someone or something looking back.

6. Underline all the sentences from the passage above that support the idea that there may be life beyond planet Earth.

Language Arts Assessment Practice (cont.)

7. The passage on page 91 includes both facts and opinions. Mark **all** the statements from the passage below that are opinions.

    Ⓐ It's a significant step on the way to finding possible life in the universe.

    Ⓑ The planet has Earthlike temperatures.

    Ⓒ Gliese 581c is located 120 trillion miles from Earth.

    Ⓓ In an infinite universe, with an infinite number of planets and stars, how could the simple reactions that lead to life happen in only one place?

    Ⓔ They showed that amino acids, the building blocks of proteins, could be formed by lightning strikes in the right kind of atmosphere.

8. What are the **two** central ideas in the passage?

    _____

    _____

    _____

9. What is the author's reason for including "The Infinite Universe" section in the text? Mark the **best** answer.

    Ⓐ To explain that the universe is extremely large

    Ⓑ To demonstrate how little we know about life on other planets

    Ⓒ To show how far away the planets are from one another

    Ⓓ To describe how much there is still to learn about the universe

Language Arts Assessment Practice (cont.)

10. Read the passage and the directions that follow.

> The lights were all turned off. This was unusual. Mom always left the porch light turned on when I came home at night. Where would Mom and Dad go at this hour? I felt angry. I was so tired from school and swim practice, and I had not even celebrated my birthday. How could my parents leave me at home alone on my birthday? I stood on the porch. It was very quiet. The house was definitely empty. Why hadn't they called? And why hadn't my brother or my friends called either? I started to open the door. When I stepped into the room, I was in for the shock of my life. I screamed and started laughing and smiling.

Analyze how the author develops and contrasts the points of view of the narrator in the text.

_____

_____

_____

_____

_____

11. The paragraphs below are from a writer's informational essay for science class. Read the paragraphs and the directions that follow.

> There are many different types of plant cells. Yet they share some common stuff not found in animal cells. These features are a *cell wall, vacuoles,* and *chloroplasts.*
>
> Like animal cells, a plant cell has a cell membrane. Unlike animal cells, outside the membrane is a tough cell wall. One of the main materials of the cell wall is cellulose. Cell walls give plants their shape. Small openings in the cell wall, called *plasmodesmata,* let things travel in and out of the cell.
>
> Vacuoles are spaces in the cell. They are surrounded by a membrane. They contain a goo called *cell sap,* that is made of water, enzymes, and other chemicals needed by the cell.
>
> Chloroplasts are in many plant cells. They contain chlorophyll. This chemical allows plants to perform photosynthesis, the process plants use to produce sugar for energy.

Underline **three** words or groups of words that are too vague or informal for a science report.

Language Arts Assessment Practice (cont.)

12. A student is writing an essay about a season for a descriptive writing class. Read a paragraph from the essay and answer the question that follows.

> I love walking to school on crisp October mornings. The sun shines through the canopy of trees overhead. The leaves display the warm hues of fall. I can never decide which color I like best—the cheerful yellows, the bold oranges, the bloody reds, or the decaying browns. Beneath my feet, the leaves that have already fallen crunch like broken bones. I walk slowly so that I can savor the glory of autumn in my neighborhood.

Which **two** descriptions do not fit with the overall style and tone of the passage?

- (A) crisp October mornings; bold oranges
- (B) warm hues; decaying browns
- (C) sun shines through; cheerful yellows
- (D) bloody reds; crunch like broken bones

---

13. A student is writing an informational essay about the metric system for math class. Read a paragraph from the essay and answer the question that follows.

> The metric system is based on groups of 10. Tens are easy to work with! And they are very predictable and convertible. For instance, let's say that you are dealing with meters, but you want to have your answer in kilometers. I run 2 kilometers every day in soccer practice. To convert, move the decimal place. One km = 1,000 m. So, if you have 1,547 meters and want to convert that into kilometers, you just move the decimal three places to the left and get 1.547 kilometers. Now think about trying to convert yards into miles. One mile = 1,760 yards, so you have to divide 1,547 by 1,760 to find out that 1,547 yards is the same as .878977273 miles! One mile also equals 5,280 feet. That is some messy math!

Which **two** details are unnecessary and should be removed from the paragraph? Underline the unnecessary sentences.

Language Arts Assessment Practice *(cont.)*

14. A student is writing an informational report on the Boston Tea Party. The student must use sources that are trustworthy and appropriate for the topic. Select the **best** source for the student to use in the report.

(A) a blog describing the benefits of green tea

(B) a cookbook about tea parties

(C) a primary source article from a newspaper

(D) an almanac from 1773

15. Read this paragraph from a student's research report and the directions that follow.

> ### How Germs Spread
> A single sneeze can propel millions of germs into the air. Hands that cover a cough still deposit germs on desks, doorknobs, and computer keyboards. Diseases spread in many other ways. We can become ill from germs in food that hasn't been handled or cooked properly. Water can also be contaminated with germs—such as protozoa—especially in poor countries.

What can you conclude from the information presented above?

_____

_____

_____

Mathematics Assessment Practice

Directions: Solve the problems.

1. A railroad tie is shaped like a rectangular prism. Find the surface area of the railroad tie.

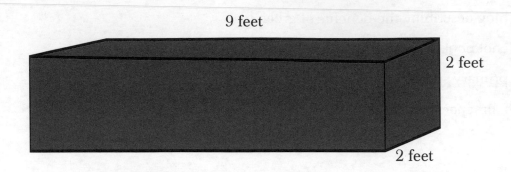

9 feet

2 feet

2 feet

2. Greg's smoothie recipe calls for $\frac{3}{4}$-cup strawberries for every 2 cups of milk. If he increases the amount of milk to 3 cups, how many cups of strawberries will he need?

          © *Teacher Created Materials*

Mathematics Assessment Practice *(cont.)*

3. Benjamin does not want to spend more than $35 on a new pair of shoes for school. Select all of the following descriptions for prices for shoes that Benjamin would buy.

   (A) 20% off a $40 pair of shoes

   (B) 25% off a $50 pair of shoes

   (C) 30% off a $40 pair of shoes with $5 shipping

   (D) A pair of $32 shoes with $4 shipping

   (E) 35% off a $40 pair of shoes with $8 shipping

   (F) 10% off a pair of $30 shoes with $8 shipping

---

4. Tanya mixes 80 gallons of paint by mixing 56 gallons of red paint with 24 gallons of white paint. Which part of every gallon is from red paint? The model represents 1 gallon of mixed paint. Color the bars to represent how much of each gallon is from red paint.

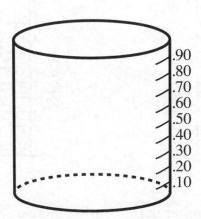

Mathematics Assessment Practice (cont.)

5. Giovanni's weekly pay rate is $465 per week. He receives a 15% raise. How can Giovanni calculate his new weekly pay rate? Mark each calculation that can correctly compute Giovanni's new weekly pay rate.

    A ($400 × .15) + ($65 × .15)

    B ($465 × 1) + ($465 × .15)

    C ($400 × 1.15) + ($65 × 1.15)

    D $465 × 15%

    E ($400 × 1.15) + ($60 × 1.15) + ($5 × 1.15)

---

6. A set contains the numbers 0, 6, 8, and 14. Two different numbers are selected randomly from this set. What is the probability that each of the given events will occur? Write a number in each box to complete the fraction that represents the probability of each event.

6a. Probability that the sum is greater than 14:

6b. Probability that the product is 0:

---

7. A basketball team is working to improve the number of baskets they make on free throws. They have been tracking their progress. These dot plots show the number of free-throw baskets each player on the team makes out of ten attempts.

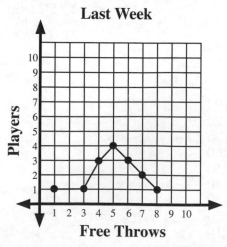

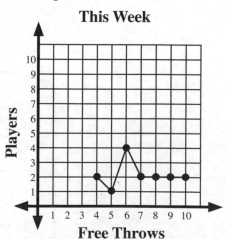

How much did the mean number of free throws increase from last week to this week? Write your answer in the box.

The mean increased by ☐ free throws.

98

#13540—Kids Learn! Getting Ready for 8th Grade

© Teacher Created Materials

Mathematics Assessment Practice (cont.)

8. This spinner has 10 equal-sized sections labeled 0, 1, 2, or 3. The arrow on the spinner is spun. Write all possible outcomes for each probability category.

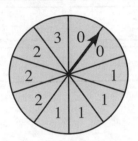

Probability Greater than $\frac{1}{4}$	Probability Less than $\frac{1}{4}$

---

9. Anabelle has $12 to spend on art supplies at the craft fair. This table shows how much each item costs at the fair. No tax is charged.

Craft Supply Prices	
Set of watercolor paints	$2.75
Set of oil pastels	$2.45
Paintbrushes	$1.35
Mounted canvas	$3.10
Modeling clay	$1.85
Scrapbooking paper	50¢ or 3 for $1.00
Easel paper	2 for 25¢

Mark all of the following combinations Anabelle could buy with her $12.

(A) 6 pieces of easel paper, 1 set of watercolor paints, 3 paintbrushes, and 1 mounted canvas

(B) 1 set of oil pastels, 2 paintbrushes, 2 mounted canvases, and 2 packages of modeling clay

(C) 9 sheets of scrapbooking paper, 1 set of watercolor paints, 1 set of oil pastels, 1 mounted canvas, and 2 paintbrushes

(D) 2 mounted canvases, 1 set of watercolor paints, and 12 sheets of easel paper

(E) 4 paintbrushes, 1 mounted canvas, and 1 set of water color paints

(F) 2 mounted canvases, 1 set of watercolor paints, and 12 sheets of scrapbooking paper

Mathematics Assessment Practice *(cont.)*

10. Write an expression in each box to make a true equation. Choose from the nine expressions in the boxes below.

10a. $-5\ \boxed{} = -5x + 25$

10b. $\frac{4}{5}\ \boxed{} = -4 + 4x$

10c. $-0.12\ \boxed{} = 0.6x + 0.6$

$(x + 5)$	$(-5x - 5)$	$(5 - 5x)$
$(5x + 5)$	$(-5x - 5x)$	$(-5 - 5x)$
$(x - 5)$	$(-x + 5)$	$(-5 + 5x)$

---

11. A representative sample of 40 students from a middle school is surveyed. The students were asked what style of art they would prefer to learn about in Art History next semester. This table shows the responses.

Style of Art	Number of Students
Cubism	12
Impressionism	8
Pop Art	2
Expressionism	4
Fauvism	14

Mark the True or False column to identify whether each statement is valid based on the survey results.

Based on the Representative Sample	True	False
11a. Six times as many students prefer cubism as prefer pop art.		
11b. In a group of 20 students, it is expected that 14 prefer fauvism.		
11c. 10% of all students prefer expressionism.		
11d. In a group of 80 students, it is expected that 24 prefer impressionism.		

© *Teacher Created Materials*

Mathematics Assessment Practice *(cont.)*

12. Solve each absolute value problem.

12a. $3 + |{-7}| = $ _____

12b. $100 - |75| = $ _____

12c. $|{-6}| + |{-42}| = $ _____

---

13. The entry fee to the used book sale is $2. Each book costs $0.75. Aynalem spent $11. How many books did she buy?

   A 12 books

   B 13 books

   C 18 books

   D 22 books

Mathematics Assessment Practice (cont.)

14. An inequality is shown.

$a \cdot b < c$

Given this inequality, write one value into each box to complete the inequalities. Assume a, b, and c are not zero.

| $-a$ | a | $-b$ | b |

14a. $a \cdot \boxed{} > -c$

14b. $\boxed{} \cdot -b < c$

---

15. The figure below is drawn to scale.

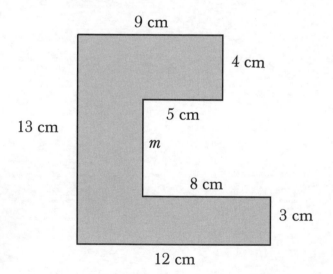

9 cm

4 cm

5 cm

13 cm

m

8 cm

3 cm

12 cm

15a. What is the length of side m? _____

15b. What is the area of the figure in cm²? _____

102

#13540—Kids Learn! Getting Ready for 8th Grade

© *Teacher Created Materials*

Great Work!

(Name)

has completed
Kids Learn! Getting Ready for 8th Grade

(Date)

Answer Key

Page 20

1. He was embarrassed to fall in front of Mr. and Mrs. Clayton, and his uniform was drenched with dirty water.
2. The large seaman believed that the captain's actions were uncalled for since the small and old sailor was simply doing his job and had no intention of harming the captain. Therefore, he became angry when his friend was hurt since he believed that the action was not just.

Page 21

1. 14
2. −0.00014
3. 0.1
4. 10
5. 30
6. 112
7. 0.18
8. 2.646
9. −37.5
10. 2.6628
11. Answers will vary. Possible answer: If an even number of factors in the problem is negative, then the product will be positive; if an odd number of factors in the problem is negative, then the product will be negative.

Page 22

Answers will vary.

Page 23

1. $-\frac{49}{4}$
2. $\frac{1}{14}$
3. $-\frac{5}{3}$
4. $-\frac{9}{4}$
5. 6.46
6. $\frac{2}{9}$
7. $2\frac{1}{16}$
8. −4

Page 23 *(cont.)*

9. 51.95
10. −6
11. The better buy is the 12-pound bag. It costs $1.50 per pound, while the 15-pound bag costs $1.60 per pound.

Page 24

Omit sentences 1 and 2. Sentence 4 can be eliminated or incorporated.

Answers will vary. Possible paragraph: The school week should be reduced to four longer days per week. I know what I'm talking about, because my dad once had a job with a four-day work week, working ten hours per day. Our family really liked it because of the extra time we spent together as a family on his three-day weekend, and my dad liked it because he didn't get burned out. Now, we teens could benefit in the same way. We could spend more time with our friends and family in a non-educational setting and have fun together, just like my family did, and we wouldn't get burned out quite so easily. Speaking of burnout, don't teachers need the same option? You get burned out just as easily as we teens do. I believe we would gladly sacrifice and go to school eight full hours a day for four days in order to have a longer weekend. After all, we teens need more rest time since we're still growing, and an extra day is all we're asking. This is not at the expense of our education because we will still put in the same amount of hours as in a five-day school week. Please consider that a four-day school week would really benefit students as well as teachers.

Page 25

1. $4y$
2. $2b$
3. $3r$
4. $-c$
5. $3b + \frac{5}{3}d$
6. $3x + 2y^3 - 4y$
7. $-2x + 3y$
8. $\frac{1}{3}$
9. 27
10. 4
11. 12
12. −20
13. 6
14. 2
15. 5

Page 26

Answers will vary. Possible answers include: The prince would describe the event from his eyes, describing the people in the crowds and what the people are wearing. The prince might feel sorry for the boy and the people in the streets. The prince might also feel less excitement and more guilt for being privileged. The story might also explain more on why the prince is upset about the treatment of the pauper.

Page 27

1. 10.1
2. 5.9
3. Answers will vary. Possible inference: The average man watches more television than the average woman.

Answer Key (cont.)

Page 28
1. a golden brooch
2. She treasures it more than any other possession she owns.
3. She could give it up if she had to.
4. She wishes she had inherited her mother's courage because she needs to be more courageous.
5. Answers will vary.

Page 29
1. 60%
2. 24 shots
3. 71%
4. 17 shots
5. 89%
6. 19 shots
7. 94%
8. 65%

Challenge: Answers will vary.

Page 30
Answers will vary.

Page 31
1. A
2. C

Page 32
1. Group A: $\frac{56}{7}$; Group B: $\frac{54}{6}$; A < B; Jade had the greater share of orange slices.
2. Group C: $\frac{27}{4}$; Group D: $\frac{39}{6}$; C > D; On average, an individual in Group C ran more than an individual in Group D.
3. Group E: $\frac{29}{12}$; Group F: $\frac{18}{8}$; Group G: $\frac{11}{4}$; Group H: $\frac{105}{36}$; Group I: $\frac{32}{12}$; Group J: $\frac{39}{18}$; J < F < E < I < G < H; The individuals in Group J received the least amount of gum.
4. Bag K: $\frac{15}{4}$; Bag L: $\frac{20}{5}$; Bag M: $\frac{25}{8}$; M < K < L; The best buy is Bag M. The worst buy is Bag L.

Page 33
Answers will vary, but should be close to the following:
1. a. The poem has four stanzas.
   b. There are five lines per stanza.
   c. ABAAB
   d. 4
2. The rhythm varies. Examples will vary.
3. Answers will vary.

Page 34
She was trying to make up her mind.

Page 35
1. capable of being heard
2. a disease that affects all countries, continents, or the world
3. inability to sleep
4. deserted
5. Answers will vary.

Page 36
1. 3.6
2. 8.0
3. 0.875
4. 6.25
5. 0.5625
6. $4.\overline{5}$
7. 321.0
8. $0.\overline{18}$
9. 1.125
10. $0.\overline{65}$

Page 37
1. Answers will vary. Possible answers: The author wrote this passage to inform readers about monkeys.
2. Answers will vary, but should provide evidence from the passage that the author likes monkeys.

Page 38
1.

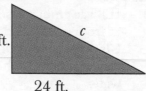

$7^2 + 24^2 = c^2$; The length of the plane is 25 feet.

2.

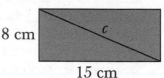

$8^2 + 15^2 = c^2$; The diagonal is 17 cm.

3.

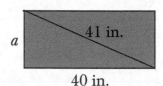

$a^2 + 40^2 = 41^2$; The height is 9 in.

4. $9^2 + b^2 = 17.5^2$; The distance across the lake is about 15 miles.

© Teacher Created Materials

Answer Key (cont.)

Page 39
Sentences will vary.
1. pipe down; The referee told the crowd to be quiet.
2. get away with anything; At basketball practice, we have to follow the rules.
3. puts his foot down; When it comes to fighting, my dad won't allow it.
4. turn my nose up; I wouldn't give up a chance to wrestle him.
5. getting cold feet; Tia is getting nervous about her audition.
6. blew his stack; Hudson became quite angry after doing poorly on his test.
7. as fit as a fiddle; My grandfather is in great shape–and he's 104 years old!
8. lost his shirt; Mr. Gordon made a bad business move and lost money.

Page 40
1.

Number of Dogs Walked (x)	Expression	Profit (in Dollars) (y)
2	$4(2) - 20$	-12
4	$4(4) - 20$	-4
6	$4(6) - 20$	4
8	$4(8) - 20$	12
10	$4(10) - 20$	20

2.

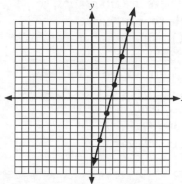

3. $y = 4x - 20$
4. 4

Page 41
Answers will vary.

Page 42
1. C
2. B
3. C

Page 43
1. Tuesday, March 25
2. Wednesday, March 19
3. Wednesday, March 12
4. Monday, February 17

Page 44
Answers will vary.

Page 45
1. 4
2. $x + 16 = 20$
3. $x = CA + FL + GA + IL + MI + NY + NC + OH + PA + TX.$
   $x = 256$
4. 282
5. 14
6. $x + y + z = 55$; Illinois, North Carolina, and Pennsylvania

Page 46
1. positive; negative
2. positive; negative
3. negative; positive
4. negative; positive
5. positive; negative
6. positive; negative
7. negative; positive
8. positive; negative
9. Answers will vary. Possible answers: thin/scrawny; bold/brazen
10. Answers will vary. Possible answers: special/different; thrifty/penny-pincher

Page 47
1. 219.8 ft.
2. 452.16 ft.^{2}
3. Answers will vary.

Page 48
Poems will vary.

Page 49
1. a. 35 yd.^{2} or 314.5 ft.^{2}
   b. $700.00
2. a. 185 ft.^{2}
   b. $125.00

Page 50
1. with the top scores; to the next round
2. from the library
3. with strawberries and cream
4. about his experience; at summer camp
5. through the mountains; to my aunt's house
6. among the trees
7. for the test
8. across the street; from the high school
9. after the earthquake; in temporary shelters
10. For some people; after memorizing common prepositions

Page 51
1. Answers will vary. Possible answer: The results will be similar, but likely not exactly the same.
2. Answers will vary. The average should be around one in six.
3. Answers will vary. The average should be around two in six (or one in three).

Page 52
Answers will vary.

Page 53
Answers will vary.

Answer Key (cont.)

Page 54
1. 84.78 cm^3
2. 254.34 cm^3
3. You would need three cone-shaped cups to hold the same amount of water of one cylindrical cup. This is apparent since the formula for a cone and cylinder are the same except for the $\frac{1}{3}$ in front of the formula for the volume of a cone.

Page 55
Answers will vary. Possible answers:
Queen/Drone:
Alike—They mate. They do not hunt for food.
Different—Queen lays eggs. Queen lives a long time.
Drone/Worker:
Alike—They do not lay eggs.
Different—Drones cannot suck nectar, but worker bees can. Drones mate, but workers do not. Drones can get kicked out of the colony.
Worker/Queen:
Alike—They live in the same colony.
Different—Workers do not lay eggs or mate. Workers hunt for food, while the Queen does not.

Page 56
1. Let s = amount to be sold, $917.26 + s \geq 1{,}200$; $s \geq 282.74$; at least $282.74
2. Let r = revenue, $r - 210 \geq 1{,}780$; $r \geq 1{,}990$; at least $1,990
3. Let a = amount to save, $4a \geq 55$; $a \geq 13.75$; at least $13.75 per week
4. Let t = total of sales, $0.16t \geq 200$; $t \geq 1250$

Page 57
Answers will vary. Possible definitions:
1. disturbance, turmoil
2. to send on assignment
3. affected or strongly stirred by emotion
4. to lay open
5. a person who empowers or authorizes
6. display
7. conforming, yielding

Page 58
1. rectangle
2. square
3. triangle
4. square
5. triangle
6. rectangle

Page 59
1. Answers will vary. Two key ideas are that the Shah Jahan loved his wife enough to have the Taj Mahal built and the explanation for how the Taj Mahal was built.
2. Summaries will vary.

Page 60
1. $32 - 40 = -8$; Forty degrees below freezing is -8 degrees.
2. $-4 + -11 + -6 = -21$; She was 21 shots below par after three rounds.
3. $-\$1{,}000 + 750 = -\$250$; $250 was still owed.
4. $-600 + 200 + 100 + 150 = -150$; The contestant needs 150 points to get back to zero.
5. $134 - (-128.6) = 262.6$; The difference between temperatures is 262.6 degrees.

Page 61
1. tell anyone
2. extremely beautiful
3. unbelievable
4. very hungry
5. make a change
6. hate
7. stick
8. avoid

Page 62
1. equilateral triangle
2. scalene triangle
3. isosceles triangle
4. isosceles triangle

Page 63
Answers will vary.

Page 64
1. Answers will vary. Possible answer: The author of this passage uses dialogue to express his or her point of view.
2. Answers will vary.
3. Answers will vary.

Page 65
1. 24
2. 1:2; $\frac{1}{2}$; 50%
3. 3:4; $\frac{3}{4}$; 75%
4. Answers will vary.

Page 66
Answers will vary.

Page 67
1a. There are no grapes, so there is no cost.
1b. One pound of grapes costs $3.00.
2a. There are no batteries.
2b. One pack of batteries has ten batteries in it.

Page 68
Answers will vary.

#13540—Kids Learn! Getting Ready for 8th Grade

© Teacher Created Materials

Answer Key (cont.)

Page 69

1. $x = (80 + 40 + 50 + 40)\ 6$
   $x = \frac{1260}{60}$
   $x = 21$ hours
2. $x = 2\ (80 + 40 + 50 + 40)\ 3$
   $x = \frac{1260}{60}$
   $x = 21$ hours

Page 70

Answers will vary. Possible answers:

1. The firefighters showed great courage and strength when they rescued people trapped in a burning building.
2. Quinn usually eats healthy foods, but chocolate is her weakness.
3. Renee set Raj up with Lana so that they could go to the dance.
4. The museum curator's investigation revealed the many illegal acts done by museum officials.

Page 71

1. The 22.5-ounce jar at $0.18 per ounce, since the 18-ounce jar costs $0.21 per ounce.
2. 0.7056 oz.
3. 43 correct; 7 incorrect
4. $13.08

Page 72

1. B
2. D
3. C
4. C

Page 73

1. $-4x - 5y$
2. $-3n$
3. $-7m + 21$
4. $8x - 20y + 6$
5. $-10a + 17b$
6. $9x - 23y$
7. $-6c + d$
8. $-3k - 18$
9. $-19m - 28$
10. $-24x + 33y$
11. $-9r^2 + 8r$
12. $-2x^2 + 16x - 12$

Page 74

Answers will vary.

Page 75

Answers will vary.

Page 76

1. $34 - (-7) = 41;\ 41°$

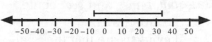

2. $-4 - (-21) = 17;\ 17°$

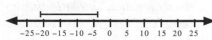

3. $-23 - (4) = -27;\ 27°$

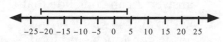

Page 77

Answers will vary.

Page 78

1. Keira: 1.6
2. Keira: $-\frac{3}{10}$
3. Malia: 3
4. Malia: 1.53
5. Answers will vary.

Page 79

Answers will vary.

Page 80

1a. $0.2x \le 15;\ x \le 75;\ \$75$
1b.

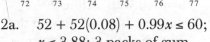

2a. $52 + 52(0.08) + 0.99x \le 60;$
    $x \le 3.88;$ 3 packs of gum
2b.

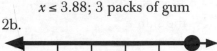

Page 81

1. Answers will vary. Possible answer: Rhubarb can be a delicious pie or a poison.
2. Answers will vary.

Page 82

1.

Sum	Probability
2	$\frac{1}{36}$
3	$\frac{1}{18}$
4	$\frac{1}{12}$
5	$\frac{1}{9}$
6	$\frac{5}{36}$
7	$\frac{1}{6}$
8	$\frac{5}{36}$
9	$\frac{1}{9}$
10	$\frac{1}{12}$
11	$\frac{1}{18}$
12	$\frac{1}{36}$

2. Outcomes will vary.
3. Answers will vary.

Page 83

Answers will vary.

Page 84

1a. $220x + 32 + 30 \ge 150;$
    $x \ge 0.4;$ at least 40%
1b. $0.4(220) = p;\ p = 88;$
    88 pages
2. Answers will vary.

Page 85

Answers will vary.

Answer Key (cont.)

Language Arts Assessment Practice

1. He helped his little sister with homework; He also assisted with setting the dinner table and mowed the lawn every weekend during the summer.

2. Answers will vary. Possible answer: The central idea of the text is that "Jumpin' Johnny" can act differently depending upon the situation. He was both responsible and mischievous. The sentences above fit into the central idea of the text because it shows the development of the idea. It shows that "Jumpin' Johnny" realizes there is a time and a place for certain behaviors.

3. Answers will vary. Possible answer: Johnny could jump high and slam the ball into the net. He could also make a shot from very far away.

4. Answers will vary. Possible answer: Assumed means to acquire, take on, or adopt.

5. B and C

6. The planet has Earthlike temperatures; They showed that amino acids, the building blocks of proteins, could be formed by lightning strikes in the right kind of atmosphere; More recent discoveries suggest that the conditions that led to life on Earth could easily occur on other planets; There is new evidence that even on Mars, there was once water.

7. A and D

8. Answers will vary. Possible answer: A central idea from the text is that scientists have discovered evidence that there may be life on other planets. Another central idea is that water and other conditions are necessary to sustain life.

9. D

10. Answers will vary. Possible answer: In the beginning of the passage the narrator is annoyed and angry. She is upset the lights are off and her parents didn't celebrate her birthday. She is asking questions as to why others didn't pay attention to her birthday. In contrast, at the end of the passage she is laughing and smiling.

11. *stuff, things,* and *goo* should be underlined.

12. B and D

13. *I run 2 kilometers every day in soccer practice; One mile also equals 5,280 feet.*

14. C

15. Answers will vary. Possible answer: I can conclude that germs spread easily through air, water, touch, and food.

Mathematics Assessment Practice

1. $SA = 2 (2 \times 2) + 4(2 \times 9) = 80$ ft.^{2}

2. $1\frac{1}{8}$-cup strawberries

3. A, C, E, and F

4.

5. B, C, and E

6a. $\frac{2}{6}$ or $\frac{1}{3}$

6b. $\frac{3}{6}$ or $\frac{1}{2}$

7. The mean increased by 1.9 free throws.

8.

Probability Greater than $\frac{1}{4}$	Probability Less than $\frac{1}{4}$
Landing on 1 Landing on 2	Landing on 0 Landing on 3

9. A, D, and E should be marked.

10a. $-5(x - 5) = -5x + 25$

10b. $\frac{4}{5} (-5 + 5x) = -4 + 4x$

10c. $-0.12(-5x - 5) = 0.6x + 0.6$

11. A and C should be marked *True*. B and D should be marked *False*.

12a. 10

12b. 25

12c. 48

13. A

14a. $-b$

14b. $-a$

15a. 6 cm

15b. 96 cm^2

#13540—Kids Learn! Getting Ready for 8th Grade
© Teacher Created Materials

Kids Learn! Parent Survey

Dear Parent,

The activities in this *Kids Learn!* book have helped your teen review grade-level skills from the recent school year and get ready for the year ahead. Your feedback on this learning resource is very valuable. Please complete the survey below and return it as directed by your teen's teacher or school administrator. Thank you in advance for your input and your time.

Please circle the term that best describes how you feel about this *Kids Learn!* book.

1. The **Introduction** (pages 4–18) gave me good ideas for things to do with my teen and offered helpful resources for extended learning.

   Strongly Agree   Agree   Disagree   Strongly Disagree

2. The **Weekly Activities for Students** (pages 20–85) were easy to understand and helped me guide my teen to complete the activity sheets. The activities were at an appropriate level of difficulty for my teen.

   Strongly Agree   Agree   Disagree   Strongly Disagree

3. The **Assessment Practice** (pages 86–102), which shows the types of questions that will be on Common Core State Standards annual assessments, gave me and my teen a better understanding of the standardized tests and how to prepare for them.

   Strongly Agree   Agree   Disagree   Strongly Disagree

4. The sections of *Kids Learn!* that were particularly helpful or useful for me and my teen were: (*Please check all that apply.*)

   ☐ Top 10 Things Your Eighth Grader Will Need to Know

   ☐ Things to Do at Home

   ☐ Things to Do in the Community

   ☐ Suggested Vacation Reading and Log

   ☐ Websites and Apps for Parents and Teens

   ☐ Weekly Activities for Students

   ☐ Preparing Your Teen for Assessments

Please provide any additional comments or suggestions about this *Kids Learn!* book.

_____

_____

_____

_____

Kids Learn! Encuesta para los padres

Querido padre de familia:

Las actividades en este libro *Kids Learn!* han ayudado a su hijo a repasar las destrezas de nivel de grado del reciente año escolar y a prepararse para el año siguiente. Sus comentarios sobre este recurso educativo son muy valiosos. Por favor, complete la encuesta a continuación y regrésela como lo indica el maestro o administrador escolar de su hijo. Le agradecemos de antemano por su participación y por su tiempo.

Por favor encierre con un círculo el término que mejor describe su opinión sobre este libro *Kids Learn!*

1. La **Introducción** (páginas 5–18) me dio buenas ideas de cosas que hacer con mi hijo y me ofrecieron recursos útiles para ampliar el aprendizaje.

    Totalmente de acuerdo   De acuerdo   En desacuerdo   Totalmente en desacuerdo

2. Las **Actividades semanales para los estudiantes** (páginas 20–85) eran fáciles de entender y me ayudaron a guiar a mi hijo a completar las hojas de ejercicios. Las actividades eran de un nivel de dificultad adecuado para mi hijo.

    Totalmente de acuerdo   De acuerdo   En desacuerdo   Totalmente en desacuerdo

3. La **Práctica para la evaluación** (páginas 86–102), muestra los tipos de preguntas que vendrán en las evaluaciones anuales de Estándares comunes del estado (*Common Core State Standards*), nos dio a mí y a mi hijo un mejor entendimiento de los exámenes estandarizados y de cómo prepararse.

    Totalmente de acuerdo   De acuerdo   En desacuerdo   Totalmente en desacuerdo

4. Las secciones de *Kids Learn!* que fueron particularmente útiles o nos ayudaron a mí y a mi hijo fueron: *(Por favor marque todas las que sean pertinentes)*.

    ☐ Las 10 cosas que su hijo de octavo grado debe saber

    ☐ Cosas para hacer en casa

    ☐ Cosas para hacer en la comunidad

    ☐ Registro de lectura y la lectura sugerida para las vacaciones

    ☐ Páginas web y aplicaciones para padres e hijos

    ☐ Actividades semanales para estudiantes

    ☐ Preparar a su hijo para las evaluaciones

Por favor proporcione cualquier comentario o sugerencia adicional sobre este libro *Kids Learn!*

_____